Complete Wedding Guide

By Donna Kooler

A LEISURE ARTS PUBLICATION

10 9 8 7 6 5 4 3 2 1

Library of Congress Cataloging-in-Publication Data
    Kooler, Donna
    Complete Wedding Guide
    "A Leisure Arts Publication"

ISBN: 1-57486-210-3

Contributors

PRODUCED BY

KOOLER DESIGN STUDIO inc.

PUBLISHED BY

LEISURE ARTS

If you have questions or comments
please contact:

LEISURE ARTS CUSTOMER SERVICE
P.O. Box 55595
Little Rock, AR 72215-9633
www.leisurearts.com

KOOLER DESIGN STUDIO, INC.
399 Taylor Blvd. Suite 104
Pleasant Hill, CA 94523
kds@koolerdesign.com

COLOR SEPARATIONS AND DIGITAL PREPRESS
ADMAC Digital Imaging, Emeryville, CA

PRINTED IN THE U.S.A. BY
R.R. Donnelley & Sons, Co.

KOOLER DESIGN STUDIO

PRESIDENT: Donna Kooler
EXECUTIVE V.P.: Linda Gillum
VICE PRESIDENT: Priscilla Timm
EDITOR: Judy Swager
ILLUSTRATORS: Linda Gillum, Barbara Baatz
Sandy Orton, Tom Taneyhill
Nancy Rossi, Jorja Hernandez
STAFF: Sara Angle, Jennifer Drake
Virginia Hanley-Rivett
Marsha Hinkson, Arlis Johnson
Karen Million, Char Randolph

COMPLETE WEDDING GUIDE

CREATIVE DIRECTOR: Donna Kooler
BOOK DESIGN: Nancy Wong Spindler
WRITER: Kit Schlich
COPY EDITORS: Joan Cravens, Judy Swager
ILLUSTRATOR: Sandy Orton
PHOTOGRAPHERS: Dianne Woods, Berkeley, CA
Don Fraser, Berkeley, CA
PHOTO STYLISTS: Donna Kooler, Basha Hanner
Ina Rice

Contents

Getting Started

WHAT A LOVELY TIME IN YOUR LIFE! AS YOU PLAN YOUR wedding, you embark on a joyful, life-changing event. It is a grand adventure during which you make decisions large and small to create a one-of-a-kind wedding, one tailored for you and your groom, a day to delight your guests.

This book, a companion to *Elegant Wedding Ceremonies, Beautiful Wedding Receptions,* and *Great Wedding Parties*, is your "hands-on" guide to help you organize all the steps you take and decisions you make as you plan your ideal wedding. Use this book to keep track of important tasks and record the information you gather about the people and services you hire to make your dreams a reality.

Good planning spares you the stress of last-minute work and helps you spend your money wisely, thus ensuring that the weeks before your wedding are as problem-free as possible.

A countdown-to-the-wedding calendar is an invaluable tool that will help you get organized, so you can glide through your preparations with ease and grace. See pages 73–90 to devise your own personal schedule and check off the tasks and decisions that are the building blocks of your dream wedding.

Establishing a master wedding budget enables you to see at a glance all the expenses you will face and helps you weigh your options. Knowing that a written budget governs your various expenses is a great reassurance. See pages 22–29 to design your budget, estimate your expenses, and record the actual costs.

Wise planning also enables you to obtain the location and services you want. Popular wedding sites, photographers, caterers, and bakers are often booked a year or more in advance, so the earlier you can set the wedding date and sign contracts with your service providers, the less likely you will be disappointed.

CHOOSING THE DATE AND CITY

SELECTING YOUR WEDDING DATE

Setting an exact wedding date depends on the availability of wedding and reception sites and your officiant's schedule. Nevertheless, you and your fiancé can think about your favorite month or season.

Keep the following things in mind when contemplating your wedding date.

❧ A formal wedding takes a minimum of six months to plan; you may need more time if you want a popular location or particular service provider. Even the most informal wedding calls for at least three months to plan. Twelve months or more is ideal for relaxed planning and optimal choices.

❧ What time of year do you like best? What season or month holds special meaning for you?

❧ Think about holidays and important family dates such as birthdays, anniversaries, other family weddings, the upcoming birth of a child, graduations, and other foreseeable family events which may conflict with your plans.

❧ Think about the hours of daylight at certain times of the year including daylight savings time.

❧ Check the availability of your prospective location.

❧ Check your prospective officiant's and attendants' schedules.

❧ Weigh the cost of holding your wedding during peak wedding season (April through October) against the cost of a non-peak month. The most popular months are June, August, and September. The most popular days of the week are Saturday, Sunday, and Friday.

SELECTING THE CITY

Choosing to marry in a nearby location makes it more convenient to plan the various elements of your wedding. Choosing the city where the groom, his parents or your parents live, provides support in that location. However, you may find it practical to hire a wedding consultant based in that city to help you arrange services such as florists and catering.

At the other end of the spectrum would be the location where you will honeymoon, a resort or vacation destination. If you have your heart set on this option, you can work with a consultant or event coordinator by phone, email, and fax. Think about travel expenses for your guests. Invite only those who could realistically attend, which will probably winnow down your guest list significantly. Consider holding a reception party at a later date closer to home, in a location convenient for all.

YOUR GUEST AND GIFT LIST

COMPOSING YOUR GUEST LIST

What comes first, your budget or your guest list? It's best to consider them together. The number of guests will determine the ceremony and reception sites you choose, and it directly affects the reception food and beverage costs. So, your budget will govern the number of guests you can serve. Begin by noting your "must-have" guests, work on a preliminary budget, then include as many guests as you can realistically serve. As a courtesy, mail out invitations (see page 31) no fewer than six weeks before the wedding date.

Regardless of who pays for the wedding, the bride's family, the groom's family, and the bridal couple generally each choose one-third of the guests, but it's natural for this ratio to vary.

KEEPING TRACK OF GIFTS

To make your record-keeping simple, this book allows you to note the gifts you receive along with the master guest list. The addresses are already in place, and you can check off the gifts you've already acknowledged with thank-you notes.

More than just a courtesy, sending thank-you notes has a practical purpose, too. Gift-givers need to know that their gifts arrived and didn't get lost in the mail or during the reception festivities. Guests are customarily allowed one full year to give gifts, but it's always a good idea to acknowledge gifts promptly. For more about thank-you notes, see page 36.

Keep track of gifts as they arrive. Because so many guests bring gifts to the reception, have a family member or one of your attendants tape cards to the packages so they won't get misplaced when packages are moved to another location.

It is not in good taste to suggest to guests that you would prefer one kind of gift (money, for example) to another, unless this information is specifically solicited.

REGISTERING AT STORES

Registering your gift preferences with department and specialty stores (including online) makes it easy for your guests to select things you have personally chosen, a "win-win" situation for everyone. After doing some preliminary comparison shopping, work with a registry consultant or online program to hone in on the things you want. Choose a variety of gifts in a wide price range.

Announcing to your guests that you have registered at a particular store is not considered proper. It is acceptable for your attendants and family members to furnish this information to guests, if asked. If you choose to register, do so well before showers and other prenuptial parties.

GUEST AND GIFT LIST

Name ....
Address ....
Tel.............................. No. attending.............
Gift ....
☐ Thank-you note sent

Name ....
Address ....
Tel.............................. No. attending.............
Gift ....
☐ Thank-you note sent

Name ....
Address ....
Tel.............................. No. attending.............
Gift ....
☐ Thank-you note sent

Name ....
Address ....
Tel.............................. No. attending.............
Gift ....
☐ Thank-you note sent

Name ....
Address ....
Tel.............................. No. attending.............
Gift ....
☐ Thank-you note sent

Name ....
Address ....
Tel.............................. No. attending.............
Gift ....
☐ Thank-you note sent

Name ....
Address ....
Tel.............................. No. attending.............
Gift ....
☐ Thank-you note sent

Name ....
Address ....
Tel.............................. No. attending.............
Gift ....
☐ Thank-you note sent

Name ....
Address ....
Tel.............................. No. attending.............
Gift ....
☐ Thank-you note sent

Name ....
Address ....
Tel.............................. No. attending.............
Gift ....
☐ Thank-you note sent

Name ....
Address ....
Tel.............................. No. attending.............
Gift ....
☐ Thank-you note sent

Name ....
Address ....
Tel.............................. No. attending.............
Gift ....
☐ Thank-you note sent

GUEST AND GIFT LIST

Name ....
Address ....
Tel .... No. attending..............
Gift ....
☐ Thank-you note sent

Name ....
Address ....
Tel .... No. attending..............
Gift ....
☐ Thank-you note sent

Name ....
Address ....
Tel .... No. attending..............
Gift ....
☐ Thank-you note sent

Name ....
Address ....
Tel .... No. attending..............
Gift ....
☐ Thank-you note sent

Name ....
Address ....
Tel .... No. attending..............
Gift ....
☐ Thank-you note sent

Name ....
Address ....
Tel .... No. attending..............
Gift ....
☐ Thank-you note sent

Name ....
Address ....
Tel .... No. attending..............
Gift ....
☐ Thank-you note sent

Name ....
Address ....
Tel .... No. attending..............
Gift ....
☐ Thank-you note sent

Name ....
Address ....
Tel .... No. attending..............
Gift ....
☐ Thank-you note sent

Name ....
Address ....
Tel .... No. attending..............
Gift ....
☐ Thank-you note sent

Name ....
Address ....
Tel .... No. attending..............
Gift ....
☐ Thank-you note sent

Name ....
Address ....
Tel .... No. attending..............
Gift ....
☐ Thank-you note sent

GUEST AND GIFT LIST

Name ....

Address ....

Tel..................................... No. attending............

Gift ....

☐ Thank-you note sent

Name ....

Address ....

Tel..................................... No. attending............

Gift ....

☐ Thank-you note sent

Name ....

Address ....

Tel..................................... No. attending............

Gift ....

☐ Thank-you note sent

Name ....

Address ....

Tel..................................... No. attending............

Gift ....

☐ Thank-you note sent

Name ....

Address ....

Tel..................................... No. attending............

Gift ....

☐ Thank-you note sent

Name ....

Address ....

Tel..................................... No. attending............

Gift ....

☐ Thank-you note sent

Name ....

Address ....

Tel..................................... No. attending............

Gift ....

☐ Thank-you note sent

Name ....

Address ....

Tel..................................... No. attending............

Gift ....

☐ Thank-you note sent

Name ....

Address ....

Tel..................................... No. attending............

Gift ....

☐ Thank-you note sent

Name ....

Address ....

Tel..................................... No. attending............

Gift ....

☐ Thank-you note sent

Name ....

Address ....

Tel..................................... No. attending............

Gift ....

☐ Thank-you note sent

Name ....

Address ....

Tel..................................... No. attending............

Gift ....

☐ Thank-you note sent

GUEST AND GIFT LIST

Name ....
Address ....
Tel .... No. attending............
Gift ....
☐ Thank-you note sent

Name ....
Address ....
Tel .... No. attending............
Gift ....
☐ Thank-you note sent

Name ....
Address ....
Tel .... No. attending............
Gift ....
☐ Thank-you note sent

Name ....
Address ....
Tel .... No. attending............
Gift ....
☐ Thank-you note sent

Name ....
Address ....
Tel .... No. attending............
Gift ....
☐ Thank-you note sent

Name ....
Address ....
Tel .... No. attending............
Gift ....
☐ Thank-you note sent

Name ....
Address ....
Tel .... No. attending............
Gift ....
☐ Thank-you note sent

Name ....
Address ....
Tel .... No. attending............
Gift ....
☐ Thank-you note sent

Name ....
Address ....
Tel .... No. attending............
Gift ....
☐ Thank-you note sent

Name ....
Address ....
Tel .... No. attending............
Gift ....
☐ Thank-you note sent

Name ....
Address ....
Tel .... No. attending............
Gift ....
☐ Thank-you note sent

Name ....
Address ....
Tel .... No. attending............
Gift ....
☐ Thank-you note sent

GUEST AND GIFT LIST

Name ....

Address ....

Tel .... No. attending..............

Gift ....

☐ Thank-you note sent

Name ....

Address ....

Tel .... No. attending..............

Gift ....

☐ Thank-you note sent

Name ....

Address ....

Tel .... No. attending..............

Gift ....

☐ Thank-you note sent

Name ....

Address ....

Tel .... No. attending..............

Gift ....

☐ Thank-you note sent

Name ....

Address ....

Tel .... No. attending..............

Gift ....

☐ Thank-you note sent

Name ....

Address ....

Tel .... No. attending..............

Gift ....

☐ Thank-you note sent

Name ....

Address ....

Tel .... No. attending..............

Gift ....

☐ Thank-you note sent

Name ....

Address ....

Tel .... No. attending..............

Gift ....

☐ Thank-you note sent

Name ....

Address ....

Tel .... No. attending..............

Gift ....

☐ Thank-you note sent

Name ....

Address ....

Tel .... No. attending..............

Gift ....

☐ Thank-you note sent

Name ....

Address ....

Tel .... No. attending..............

Gift ....

☐ Thank-you note sent

Name ....

Address ....

Tel .... No. attending..............

Gift ....

☐ Thank-you note sent

GUEST AND GIFT LIST

Name ....

Address ....

Tel.................................. No. attending.............

Gift ....

☐ Thank-you note sent

Name ....

Address ....

Tel.................................. No. attending.............

Gift ....

☐ Thank-you note sent

Name ....

Address ....

Tel.................................. No. attending.............

Gift ....

☐ Thank-you note sent

Name ....

Address ....

Tel.................................. No. attending.............

Gift ....

☐ Thank-you note sent

Name ....

Address ....

Tel.................................. No. attending.............

Gift ....

☐ Thank-you note sent

Name ....

Address ....

Tel.................................. No. attending.............

Gift ....

☐ Thank-you note sent

Name ....

Address ....

Tel.................................. No. attending.............

Gift ....

☐ Thank-you note sent

Name ....

Address ....

Tel.................................. No. attending.............

Gift ....

☐ Thank-you note sent

Name ....

Address ....

Tel.................................. No. attending.............

Gift ....

☐ Thank-you note sent

Name ....

Address ....

Tel.................................. No. attending.............

Gift ....

☐ Thank-you note sent

Name ....

Address ....

Tel.................................. No. attending.............

Gift ....

☐ Thank-you note sent

Name ....

Address ....

Tel.................................. No. attending.............

Gift ....

☐ Thank-you note sent

GUEST AND GIFT LIST

Name ....

Address ....

Tel .... No. attending ....

Gift ....

☐ Thank-you note sent

Name ....

Address ....

Tel .... No. attending ....

Gift ....

☐ Thank-you note sent

Name ....

Address ....

Tel .... No. attending ....

Gift ....

☐ Thank-you note sent

Name ....

Address ....

Tel .... No. attending ....

Gift ....

☐ Thank-you note sent

Name ....

Address ....

Tel .... No. attending ....

Gift ....

☐ Thank-you note sent

Name ....

Address ....

Tel .... No. attending ....

Gift ....

☐ Thank-you note sent

Name ....

Address ....

Tel .... No. attending ....

Gift ....

☐ Thank-you note sent

Name ....

Address ....

Tel .... No. attending ....

Gift ....

☐ Thank-you note sent

Name ....

Address ....

Tel .... No. attending ....

Gift ....

☐ Thank-you note sent

Name ....

Address ....

Tel .... No. attending ....

Gift ....

☐ Thank-you note sent

Name ....

Address ....

Tel .... No. attending ....

Gift ....

☐ Thank-you note sent

Name ....

Address ....

Tel .... No. attending ....

Gift ....

☐ Thank-you note sent

GIFTS FROM THOSE NOT ON YOUR GUEST LIST

Name ....
Address ....
Gift ....
☐ Thank-you note sent

Name ....
Address ....
Gift ....
☐ Thank-you note sent

Name ....
Address ....
Gift ....
☐ Thank-you note sent

Name ....
Address ....
Gift ....
☐ Thank-you note sent

Name ....
Address ....
Gift ....
☐ Thank-you note sent

Name ....
Address ....
Gift ....
☐ Thank-you note sent

Name ....
Address ....
Gift ....
☐ Thank-you note sent

Name ....
Address ....
Gift ....
☐ Thank-you note sent

Name ....
Address ....
Gift ....
☐ Thank-you note sent

Name ....
Address ....
Gift ....
☐ Thank-you note sent

Name ....
Address ....
Gift ....
☐ Thank-you note sent

Name ....
Address ....
Gift ....
☐ Thank-you note sent

Name ....
Address ....
Gift ....
☐ Thank-you note sent

Name ....
Address ....
Gift ....
☐ Thank-you note sent

YOUR WEDDING PARTY

FAMILY AND FRIENDS

Your wedding is a wonderful opportunity to bring your family and friends together in a shared endeavor. Identify individuals among them with special talents or resources, and invite them to help you with your wedding preparations. Discuss responsibilities thoroughly with each helper and assign deadlines.

Here are some ways in which everyone can help you:

❧ Provide the ceremony or reception site

❧ Decorate the ceremony and reception sites

❧ Design and hand-letter your invitations and other printed materials

❧ Make wedding favors

❧ Keep track of wedding gifts

❧ Perform music for your ceremony and reception

❧ Videotape your ceremony and reception

❧ Take informal photographs

❧ Provide a "getaway" site for your honeymoon

If you are not hiring the services of a wedding consultant, select a family member or friend to be your wedding day "director" to take charge of the day's events according to your timeline. Ask him or her to work directly with service providers (site manager, florist, musicians or disk jockey, caterer, bartender, baker, etc.) to make sure the events remain on schedule. Refer them to your Wedding Day Timeline on page 90.

"Director"...

Tel..

Responsibilities..

....

....

....

Special helper...

Tel..

Responsibilities..

....

Special helper...

Tel..

Responsibilities..

....

Special helper...

Tel..

Responsibilities..

....

Special helper...

Tel..

Responsibilities..

....

FINANCIAL RESPONSIBILITIES

Also see page 22.

BRIDE AND BRIDE'S FAMILY

- Engagement party
- Wedding consultant's fee
- Bride's gown, veil, and accessories
- Wedding stationery, calligraphy, and postage
- Wedding gift for the bridal couple
- Groom's wedding ring
- Bridesmaids' bouquets and gifts
- Bridesmaids' luncheon
- Photography and videography
- Bride's medical exam and blood test
- Cost of the ceremony, including site, flowers, music, and rented items
- Cost of the reception, including location, flowers, music, rented items, food, beverages, cake, decorations, favors, and guest book
- Transportation for bridal party to the ceremony and reception
- Their own attire and travel expenses

GROOM AND GROOM'S FAMILY

- Their own attire and travel expenses
- Wedding gift for the bridal couple
- Bride's wedding ring
- Gifts for the groomsmen
- Groom's medical exam and blood test
- Bride's bouquet and going-away corsage
- Mothers' and grandmothers' corsages
- All boutonnieres
- Officiant's fee
- Marriage license
- Honeymoon expenses

ATTENDANTS

- Their own attire except flowers (also see page 22)
- Travel expenses
- Bridal shower (bride's attendants)
- Bachelor party (best man, ushers)

TRADITIONAL DUTIES

HONOR ATTENDANT

- Helps the bride dress for the ceremony and arranges the bride's veil and train for the procession
- Organizes the bride's other attendants
- Plans the bridal shower
- Holds the bride's bouquet and groom's ring during the ceremony
- Signs the marriage certificate as a witness
- May help the bride choose her gown, record wedding gifts, run errands, and assist as needed

BRIDESMAIDS

- Help the honor attendant plan bridal shower
- Help the bride keep a gift record at the bridal shower
- Encourage single women to gather for the bride's bouquet toss
- Make themselves available to help the bride

BEST MAN

- Plans the bachelor party
- Helps the groom dress for the ceremony
- Organizes the groomsmen
- Holds the bride's ring during the ceremony
- Signs the marriage certificate as a witness, brings the certificate to the ceremony
- Pays the officiant, musicians, and other service providers on the day of the wedding (payment provided by couple or couple's families)
- Offers first toast at reception
- Handles the honeymoon luggage and tickets, helps the couple make their exit
- Oversees the return of rented formal wear for the groom and groomsmen

GROOMSMEN

- Help the best man plan the bachelor party
- Assist with set-up of chairs for the ceremony
- Escort guests to their seats at ceremony
- Assist guests with parking and directions

BRIDE'S ATTENDANTS

HONOR ATTENDANT
(MAID OR MATRON OF HONOR)

Name...

Address...

Tel..

Responsibilities ....

....

....

Notes ....

Name...

Address...

Tel..

Responsibilities ....

....

....

Notes ....

BRIDESMAIDS

Name...

Address...

Tel..

Responsibilities ....

....

....

Notes ....

Name...

Address...

Tel..

Responsibilities ....

....

....

Notes ....

Name...

Address...

Tel..

Responsibilities ....

....

....

Notes ....

Name...

Address...

Tel..

Responsibilities ....

....

....

Notes ....

Name...

Address...

Tel..

Responsibilities ....

....

....

Notes ....

FLOWER GIRL

Name...

Address...

Tel..

Responsibilities ....

....

....

Notes ....

GROOM'S ATTENDANTS

BEST MAN

Name ....
Address ....
Tel ....
Responsibilities ....
....
....
Notes ....

Name ....
Address ....
Tel ....
Responsibilities ....
....
....
Notes ....

GROOMSMEN

Name ....
Address ....
Tel ....
Responsibilities ....
....
....
Notes ....

Name ....
Address ....
Tel ....
Responsibilities ....
....
....
Notes ....

Name ....
Address ....
Tel ....
Responsibilities ....
....
....
Notes ....

Name ....
Address ....
Tel ....
Responsibilities ....
....
....
Notes ....

Name ....
Address ....
Tel ....
Responsibilities ....
....
....
Notes ....

RING BEARER

Name ....
Address ....
Tel ....
Responsibilities ....
....
Notes ....

Your Wedding Budget

Creating a realistic budget is one of the best wedding gifts you can give yourself. Along with the personal schedule you will develop (see page 73), a budget will organize and streamline your wedding planning in a way that eliminates unexpected expenses and unpleasant surprises. You owe it to yourself to make the adventure of planning as easy as possible so you will be relaxed and radiant on your wedding day.

Take these steps for worry-free planning:

❧ Analyze how much money you have to spend on your wedding (see below).

❧ Decide what's most important to you and allocate your expenses accordingly (see next page).

❧ Shop around for bridal services to compare costs: attend bridal fairs, thumb through bridal magazines, visit bridal websites, make telephone inquiries, and seek word-of-mouth recommendations from friends and recent brides you know.

❧ Fill in your estimated costs on the Budget Worksheet and Record (pages 24–29).

❧ Make your final decisions, sign contracts, and let the festivities begin!

HOW MUCH DO YOU HAVE TO SPEND?

Of all the elements you must weigh and evaluate as you plan your wedding, none is more personal or more essential than determining how much you have to spend. This knowledge will give you the power to make decisions with confidence. It's important to think about this early in your planning, before you go shopping for services and purchases.

In the past, tradition strictly defined who pays for specific expenses (see page 19), but this is often no longer the case. For example, a bride with an ample budget may elect to purchase dresses for her attendants, which would be an especially gracious gesture. The groom's parents may make substantial contributions to expenses listed for the bride and bride's family. Couples who have the financial ability to pay for all their own wedding expenses often choose this option. Nevertheless, it makes sense to gently sound out both families to see if they would like to make a contribution to your wedding expenses.

Build your budget from the following sources:

❧ A percentage of your current savings

❧ A percentage of your groom's current savings

❧ Current income (between now and the wedding) that the two of you can allocate for the wedding

❧ Contributions from parents or other relatives

My wedding budget from all sources is: $ ....

BUDGET ALLOCATIONS

This is the perfect time to see what wedding expenses you can avoid. You may know someone who would like to help by providing the site for the ceremony or reception, for example. Or adjust the budget in other ways.

If you plan to wear your mother's wedding dress, for example, your expenses under the heading "Bride's Attire" on the budget worksheet (page 25) may include only shoes and accessories. Consequently, you can spend a greater portion of your budget on flowers if you wish. You would then lower the percentage listed after "Bride and groom's attire" (next page) and add the difference to the percentage listed after "Flowers and decorations."

The length of your guest list directly affects the cost of food and beverages, as well as rented items such as chairs and even the size of the reception site. Begin with your ideal guest list, then winnow it down later if you must.

The following percentages are based on an average wedding. Alter the ratios to suit your needs and preferences. Just be sure the percentages add up to 100.

Budget Allocation

Category	Average Percentage	Your Estimated Expense
Pre-wedding parties	3%	TB x .03 = $
Invitations, stationery, and postage	2%	TB x .02 = $
Ceremony site and officiant	3%	TB x .03 = $
Wedding rings	3%	TB x .03 = $
Bride and groom's attire	11%	TB x .11 = $
Photography and videography	8%	TB x .08 = $
Reception site, including rentals	8%	TB x .08 = $
Flowers and decorations	6%	TB x .06 = $
Food, beverage, and cake	40%	TB x .40 = $
Music	8%	TB x .08 = $
Transportation and parking	1%	TB x .01 = $
Gifts	2%	TB x .02 = $
Incidentals	5%	TB x .05 = $
GRAND TOTAL	**100%**	Should = your total budget $

(TB = total amount of your budget; see page 22)

❧ Please note that this list does not include expenses for the honeymoon because this varies greatly from couple to couple.

❧ Also not mentioned is the fee for a wedding consultant, which may be based on either a flat hourly rate or a percentage (10%–15%) of the total cost of the services the consultant arranges for you.

Your Budget Worksheet and Record

Not all entries in the budget worksheet may pertain to your
wedding. Simply cross out those entries that do not apply.

	ESTIMATED COST	ACTUAL COST (INCL. SALES TAX)	DEPOSIT	BALANCE DUE	PAID
PRE-WEDDING PARTIES					
ENGAGEMENT PARTY					
Site rental					
Invitations					
Food and beverage					
Decorations and flowers					
Favors					
BRIDESMAIDS' LUNCHEON					
Site rental					
Invitations					
Food and beverage					
Decorations and flowers					
Favors					
REHEARSAL DINNER					
Site rental					
Invitations					
Food and beverage					
Decorations and flowers					
Favors					
Pre-wedding Parties Subtotal			*Compare to Allocation on p. 23*		
INVITATIONS, ETC.					
Invitations (incl. reply cards)					
Announcements					
Calligrapher					
Ceremony programs					
Thank-you notes					
Postage					
Invitations Subtotal			*Compare to Allocation on p. 23*		

YOUR BUDGET WORKSHEET AND RECORD

	ESTIMATED COST	ACTUAL COST (INCL. SALES TAX)	DEPOSIT	BALANCE DUE	PAID
THE CEREMONY					
Officiant's fee					
Location fee					
Tip for site manager					
Rentals: Chairs					
Arch					
Other					
Donation to church (optional)					
The Ceremony Subtotal			*Compare to Allocation on p. 23*		
RINGS					
Bride's ring					
Groom's ring					
Rings Subtotal			*Compare to Allocation on p. 23*		
ATTIRE					
Bride: Bridal gown					
Alterations					
Headpiece/veil					
Lingerie and hosiery					
Shoes					
Jewelry					
Hairdresser					
Cosmetics					
Going-away outfit					
Honeymoon clothes					
Groom: Tuxedo or suit					
Shoes					
Going-away outfit					
Honeymoon clothes					
Attire Subtotal			*Compare to Allocation on p. 23*		

Your Budget Worksheet and Record

Not all entries in the budget worksheet may pertain to your wedding. Simply cross out those entries that do not apply.

	ESTIMATED COST	ACTUAL COST (INCL. SALES TAX)	DEPOSIT	BALANCE DUE	PAID
PHOTOGRAPHY AND VIDEOGRAPHY					
Photographer's fee					
Engagement portrait					
Wedding portrait					
Wedding proofs					
Wedding prints					
Album					
Parents' albums					
Extra prints					
Videographer's fee					
Videotape					
Photography and Videography Subtotal			*Compare to Allocation on p. 23*		
RECEPTION LOCATION					
Location fee					
Tip for site manager					
EQUIPMENT RENTAL					
Tent					
Chairs					
Fans					
Heaters					
Other					
Reception Location Subtotal			*Compare to Allocation on p. 23*		

	ESTIMATED COST	ACTUAL COST (INCL. SALES TAX)	DEPOSIT	BALANCE DUE	PAID
FLOWERS AND DECORATIONS					
CEREMONY					
Flowers for decór					
Bride's bouquet					
Bridesmaids' bouquets					
Boutonnieres					
Corsages					
Other decorations					
Potted plants (rent or buy)					
Aisle runner					
RECEPTION					
Flowers for decór					
Flowers for cake					
Other decorations					
Potted plants (rent or buy)					
EXTRAS					
Place cards					
Printed napkins					
Toasting glasses					
Favors					
Guest book and pen					
Disposable cameras					
Flowers and Decorations Subtotal			*Compare to Allocation on p. 23*		

TIPPING GUIDELINES

Tipping (for the caterer and site manager) may or may not be included in service contracts, so read carefully before signing. Photographers, florists, and bakers are generally not tipped. Officiants are never tipped, although they may ask for a small donation for their house of worship if the ceremony is held on that site.

Expect to pay:

- 15–20 percent tips for caterers, reception site managers, wait staff, bartenders, limousine drivers, disk jockeys
- $1–$2 per guest (or car) for coat check, restroom, and parking attendants
- $25 tip per band member

	ESTIMATED COST	ACTUAL COST (INCL. SALES TAX)	DEPOSIT	BALANCE DUE	PAID
FOOD AND DRINK					
CAKE					
Wedding cake					
Cake topper					
Cake knife					
Cake cutting fee					
BEVERAGES					
Champagne					
Wine, including corkage fee					
Liquor					
Soft drinks, coffee, tea					
FOOD					
Hors d'oeuvres					
Entrees					
Dessert					
PERSONNEL					
Bartender					
Wait staff					
Tips for bartender and wait staff					
Tip for caterer					
EQUIPMENT RENTAL					
Linens					
Glassware					
Dinnerware					
Flatware					
Food and Drink Subtotal			*Compare to Allocation on p. 23*		
MUSIC					
Musician(s) for ceremony					
Tip for ceremony musician(s)					
Musicians for cocktail hour					
Live band or DJ for reception					
Tips for reception musicians or DJ					
Music Subtotal			*Compare to Allocation on p. 23*		

	ESTIMATED COST	ACTUAL COST (INCL. SALES TAX)	DEPOSIT	BALANCE DUE	PAID
TRANSPORTATION					
Parking					
Limousine or car rental					
Tip for limousine driver					
Specialty transportation					
Transportation Subtotal			*Compare to Allocation on p. 23*		
GIFTS					
For bride's attendants					
For groomsmen					
For bride (from groom)					
For groom (from bride)					
For parents					
For special helpers					
Gifts Subtotal			*Compare to Allocation on p. 23*		
INCIDENTAL EXPENSES					
Marriage license					
Blood tests					
Other					
Incidental Expenses Subtotal			*Compare to Allocation on p. 23*		
GRAND TOTAL					
Check this against your Grand Total figure on page 23.					

EXPENSES BEYOND YOUR BASIC WEDDING BUDGET

	ESTIMATED COST	ACTUAL COST (INCL. SALES TAX)	DEPOSIT	BALANCE DUE	PAID
HONEYMOON					
Transportation					
Accommodations					
Meals					
Spending Money					
Honeymoon Subtotal					
WEDDING CONSULTANT					

Mrs. Diane Koett
Mr. Ronald Koett
request the pleasure of your company
at the marriage of their daughter
Nicole Marie
to
Mr. Michael Gregory Blagden
Sunday, the twenty-second of August
Nineteen hundred and ninety-nine
at twelve o'clock
Piedmont Community Center
711 Highland Avenue
Piedmont, California

Reception immediately following the ceremony

Printed Matters

Whether you visit a stationery shop or browse the internet, the array of contemporary invitation styles will dazzle your eyes as you choose each individual element— the paper, typeface, images, and printing method. To acquaint yourself with various styles, ask to browse the samples at your local stationery store. Our companion book, *Elegant Wedding Ceremonies* features a gallery of contemporary favorites.

WHAT YOU NEED

INVITATIONS

At their most formal, invitations are engraved, with an inner envelope for the invitation itself and the entire suite of invitation materials, and a larger, outer envelope which you will address. The most casual may feature hand-lettering on plain paper or a museum-quality greeting card with a single envelope.

RESPONSE CARDS

These small enclosures make it easy for your guests to let you know whether they plan to attend (your caterer needs to know), and include already-stamped envelopes printed or hand-lettered with your address (or the address of the person keeping track of RSVPs). Another option is to include pre-addressed postcards, which require less postage.

ANNOUNCEMENTS

Worded similarly to your invitation, announcements are intended for people not invited to the wedding for various reasons, such as distant relatives or business associates.

THANK-YOU NOTES

The most formal are custom-printed with your new married name or monogram, in the style of your invitations. The most casual are simple, boxed note cards in any style you like.

OTHER OPTIONS

RECEPTION CARDS

These are essential if you are not inviting all wedding guests to the reception. If all are invited, you may state this at the bottom of the invitation and omit this card.

MAPS

Street maps directing your guests to your wedding and reception sites are a thoughtful courtesy. You may have these printed, but photocopies are acceptable. For best results, draw the map (or have someone else draw it) showing the simplest route(s) necessary.

WEDDING PROGRAMS

Another courtesy for your guests (and optional), a ceremony program lists the order of events, titles of the musical numbers, names of the participants, and other text of your choice. For a sample program, see page 35.

PLACE/SEATING CARDS

For planning the seating arrangement at a formal reception, these cards assign each of your guests to a specific table and seat. They may be printed or elegantly hand-lettered. See the companion book, *Beautiful Wedding Receptions* for creative and decorative ideas.

PRINTING METHODS

❧ Engraving is the most formal, elegant, and costly; it features raised letters that are "stamped" from the back by a metal plate created by the printer.

❧ Thermography is very popular and closely resembles engraving but is less expensive, the result of a heat process that fuses ink and powder into letters that are raised on the front only.

❧ Offset printing (flat printing) works well for informal invitations and when time and money are limited; it is good for hand lettering such as calligraphy and allows more than one ink color. A rubber cylinder transfers inked letters onto paper.

❧ Computer laser printing is perfect for invitations designed electronically. Avoid ink-jet printing, which runs when the ink is dampened.

INVITATIONS—WORDING

Keep this sequence in mind when wording your invitation: host, request, bride and groom, date, time, and location. Optional information (reception, fancy dress, etc.) follows at the bottom. The wording should indicate parental relationships as clearly as possible. The spellings "honour" and "favour" are customary but discretionary.

When hosted by the bride's parents:

Mr. and Mrs. William Russell
request the honour of your presence
at the marriage of their daughter
Rose Evelyn
to
Julian James Young
Saturday the sixteenth of June
two thousand and one
at six o'clock in the evening
Church of the Oaks
Westwood, California
Reception immediately following
at the Westwood Country Club
(the last two lines are optional)

Including the groom's parents as a courtesy:

Mr. and Mrs. William Russell
request the honour of your presence
at the marriage of their daughter
Rose Evelyn
to
Julian James
son of
Mr. and Mrs. Jonathan Young
etc.

When hosted by a widow who has not remarried:

Mrs. William Russell
requests the honour of your presence
at the marriage of her daughter
Rose Evelyn
etc.

When hosted by a widower who has not remarried:

Mr. William Russell
requests the honour of your presence
at the marriage of his daughter
Rose Evelyn
etc.

When hosted by the bride's mother who has remarried after being widowed or divorced:

Mr. and Mrs. Charles O'Brien
request the honour of your presence
at the marriage of Mrs. O'Brien's daughter
Rose Evelyn Russell
etc.

When hosted by the bride's father who has remarried after being widowed or divorced:

Mr. and Mrs. William Russell
request the honour of your presence
at the marriage of Mr. Russell's daughter
Rose Evelyn
etc.

When hosted by the bride's mother who is divorced but not remarried:

Mrs. Vera Russell
requests the honour of your presence
at the marriage of her daughter
Rose Evelyn
etc.

When co-hosted by the bride's parents who are divorced and remarried:

Mr. and Mrs. Stephen Chen
and
Mr. and Mrs. William Russell
request the honour of your presence
at the marriage of
Rose Evelyn Russell
etc.

When hosted by the bride's divorced, unmarried parents:

Mrs. Vera Russell
And
Mr. William Russell
request the honour of your presence
at the marriage of their daughter
Rose Evelyn
etc.

When hosted by the groom's parents:

Mr. and Mrs. Jonathan Young
request the honour of your presence
at the marriage of
Rose Evelyn Russell
to their son
Julian James Young
etc.

When co-hosted by the bride's and groom's parents:

Mr. and Mrs. William Russell
and
Mr. and Mrs. Jonathan Young
request the honour of your presence
at the marriage of their children
Rose Evelyn Russell
and Julian James Young

etc.

When hosted by the bride and groom:

The honour of your presence
is requested at the marriage of
Rose Evelyn Russell
to
Julian James Young

etc.

You may, of course, encounter other situations calling for special wording. An experienced printer or stationer can guide you.

RECEPTION CARD—WORDING

Reception Immediately following the ceremony
Westwood Country Club
1442 Quail Run
Westwood, California

RESPONSE CARD—WORDING

The favour of a reply is requested
Before the second of June
M ....
Will ....*attend*

SENDING THE INVITATIONS

ADDRESSING THE ENVELOPES

❧ Try to obtain envelopes from the stationer early, to address ahead of time.

❧ When ordering, consider having your return address printed on the flap of the outer envelope to save you time when addressing.

❧ Always hand-letter names and addresses; avoid typing or using computer-generated labels. Consider hiring a calligrapher.

❧ Avoid abbreviations except for Mr., Mrs., Ms., and state names.

❧ On the inner envelope, hand-letter only the names of the guests.

❧ When inviting a single guest, address the outer envelope with his or her name only; include the phrase "and guest" after the name when you letter the inner envelope, if desired.

ASSEMBLING THE INVITATION ENVELOPE

Proceed in this order:

❧ Place a stamp on the response card envelope.

❧ Place the response card face-up under the flap of the response card envelope.

❧ Place the response card with envelope and other optional items such as reception card and map inside the invitation, face up.

❧ Place tissue paper over the lettering on the invitation (optional).

❧ Insert the invitation face up inside the inner envelope; do not seal.

❧ Insert the inner envelope into the outer envelope with the handwritten name(s) facing the back of the outer envelope.

❧ Seal the outer envelope.

❧ Weigh the filled envelope. If it exceeds one ounce, add extra postage. (Ask a postal clerk for the correct amount.)

MAILING THE INVITATIONS

The general rule is to mail the invitations six weeks before the wedding date. Some brides allow more time if the wedding occurs over a holiday weekend or if important guests who live a great distance will have to make travel plans. It is acceptable to mail invitations fewer than six weeks before the wedding if you've had only a few months to plan.

The Wedding Celebration of
Rose Evelyn Russell
and
Julian James Young

June 16, 2001
Church of the Oaks
Westwood, California

CELEBRANT (OR OFFICIANT)
Rev. Gerald Wilson

WEDDING PARTY

| *Maid of Honor* | *Best Man* |
| Deborah Klein | Adam Schultz |

Bridesmaids	*Groomsmen*
Anna Cafasso	Vincent Kirby
Amy Hatheway	Christopher Burks
Nancy Mueller	Joseph Aurelia
Joanna Sorensen	Dan McDermott

READER
Patrick Kirk

MUSIC
The Schola Quintet

SAMPLE WEDDING PROGRAM

Programs for your wedding ceremony are optional. They make a lovely touch if your religious ceremony may be unfamiliar to some of your guests, or simply if you want them to know who comprises your bridal party, who the musicians are, and what pieces they will perform. It is acceptable to print your programs by offset printing or on a computer.

Depending on your needs, you may either design a one-column program of events to run on a single page, or plan a two-column program of personnel and events that folds in half lengthwise. For a two-page program, you may add a second, decorative page to serve as a cover for the printed program. You may want to add more pages to explain religious traditions, or print poetry or other text meaningful to the bride and groom such as remembrances or acknowledgments.

PRELUDE
Water Music
Handel

PROCESSIONAL
Trumpet Tune
Purcell

Opening Remarks
Reading

INTERLUDE
Where'er You Walk
Handel

Exchange of Vows
Blessing
Exchange of Rings
Lighting the Unity Candle

RECESSIONAL
Badinerie, Orchestral Suite No. 2
J.S. Bach

THANK-YOU NOTES

Custom and courtesy require that you acknowledge gifts promptly, ideally within one month after you return from your honeymoon. If you have a large guest list and feel overwhelmed by the task, try these two strategies:

❧ Enlist your husband to help you. Perhaps he can write notes to those guests his family invited, especially if you do not know them well.

❧ Gifts will arrive before your wedding date. Have note cards ready and write your thank-yous as the gifts arrive, or sit down once a week and write up that week's batch.

Thank-you notes need not be long or wordy, but should convey personal warmth and gratitude. Traditional thank-you notes are always handwritten, and include:

❧ A salutation such as "Dear Mr. and Mrs. Smith" (formal) or "Dear Deanna and David" (less formal)

❧ Thanks and acknowledgment of the gift. The gift-giver deserves assurance that the package reached you and that you know who sent it.

❧ Briefly mention how you will use and enjoy the gift.

❧ Additional personal comment(s): "How nice it was to see you at our wedding." "I look forward to sharing our honeymoon photos with you." "Thanks for making our wedding special."

❧ A second "thank you" is optional.

❧ Sign off with a closing such as "Sincerely" (if you don't know the giver well), "Fondly," "Affectionately," or "Love" (reserve for the closest friends and relatives).

❧ Sign only your name, but be sure to mention your spouse's name in the body of the note.

Even with these guidelines, you may still find yourself at a loss for words. What if you don't particularly like a gift, and don't know what to say? Courtesy requires that you find a pleasant way to mention the gift, whether it suits your style or not. Tap into your inventive imagination and keep the message light and gracious. What if you don't even know what the gift is or how it's supposed to be used? Ask someone (other than the giver) if they can help you, perhaps a family member, or if necessary, a store clerk.

SAMPLE THANK-YOU NOTES

An informal note to close friends:

Dear Deanna and David,

Thank you for the lovely damask tablecloth and napkins. The color is exquisite and blends with our dinnerware so well. Julian and I shall use them at dinners for our favorite friends. You can be assured you will receive an invitation as soon as we are settled in!

Thanks again for thinking of us on our special day.

Fondly,

Rose

A more formal note, perhaps to a couple your parents invited:

Dear Mr. and Mrs. Smith

Thank you so much for the generous check you gave us for our wedding. Julian and I are still furnishing our new house, and your gift will enable us to buy one of the items on our list. What a thoughtful gift for newlyweds!

I'm so glad I was finally able to meet you at our reception. Again, many thanks.

Sincerely,

Rose Russell Young

In response to a gift you don't care for:

Dear Laurie and Tom,

Thank you so much for the velvet Victorian crazy quilt you gave us for our wedding. Julian and I appreciate its fine workmanship. It will be a comfort on chilly nights.

I was delighted to see you at the wedding. I'm so glad we've kept in touch over the years, but seeing you in person was a treat.

Thanks for the warmth of your friendship.

Affectionately,

Rose

YOUR STATIONERY WORKSHEET

QUESTIONS TO ASK PROSPECTIVE STATIONERS OR PRINTERS

✂ Do you have sample books I may browse through?

✂ How long will it take to fill the order once I place it?

✂ Can I see a proof of the invitation before it's printed?

✂ What happens if there are mistakes on the order?

✂ Can I have a guarantee that my wording will remain exactly as I wrote it?

✂ Do you offer a discount if I have all my stationery (invitations, announcements, response cards, programs, napkins, match books) printed here?

Proofread the invitation information very carefully on your original order and the first printed proof.

Remember: You won't need one invitation for each guest, only one invitation per couple, family, or household. Order at least an extra dozen (or more) for last-minute invites, mistakes, and keepsakes.

You can order printed stationery from a printer, stationer, computer and calligraphy service, and off the internet. You can also buy software to create your own invitations.

Your Stationer or Printer ....

Address ....

Contact ....

Tel ....

Order placed (date) .... Est. completion date ....

Deposit $ .... Balance due $ ....

Enter the expenses on your budget worksheet on page 24.

	# Needed	Estimate $	Ordered	Addressed	Mailed
Invitations					
Professionally printed	....	....	☐	☐	☐
Or hand-made: materials	....	....	☐	☐	☐
Envelopes					
For invitations	....	....	☐	☐	☐
For all papers	....	....	☐	☐	☐
Reception Cards	....	....	☐	☐	☐
Response cards and envelopes	....	....	☐	☐	☐
(or postcards)					
Maps	....	....	☐	☐	☐
Wedding programs	....	....	☐	☐	☐
Place/Seating cards	....	....	☐	☐	☐
Announcements					
Professionally printed	....	....	☐	☐	☐
Or hand-made: materials	....	....	☐	☐	☐
Envelopes	....	....	☐	☐	☐
Thank-you notes	....	....	☐	☐	☐

YOUR CEREMONY

CHOOSING THE OFFICIANT

Questions to ask as you interview prospective officiants:

❧ Are you available on the date and at the time we plan on getting married?

❧ Would you be willing to perform the ceremony at a location other than your church?

❧ May we write our own vows?

❧ Can family members or friends take part in the ceremony (readings, music, etc.)?

❧ Does your church have an organ and organist? May we use other musicians?

❧ What is your fee?

❧ What is the standard donation for using your church?

❧ Does your church require premarital counseling?

❧ For interfaith weddings: Do you allow interfaith weddings? Do you allow participation of an additional officiant of a different faith?

❧ If not affiliated with the officiant's religion: Are there any requirements for marrying in your church?

❧ Ask yourselves: Are you comfortable with this officiant?

Prospective officiant #1..

Tel..

Comments...

Fee(s) $ ....

Prospective officiant #2..

Tel..

Comments...

Fee(s) $ ....

Prospective officiant #3..

Tel..

Comments...

Fee(s) $ ....

When you make your choice, enter the expense in Your Budget Worksheet on page 25.

YOUR VOWS

In your search for meaningful vows, look to vows traditional within your religious affiliation, scripture, and poetry. Check your library or bookstore for books of wedding vows. If you're so inclined, compose your own words for an intimately personal statement (verify with your officiant that this is acceptable).

Use the space below to record the vows you select or write. Make photocopies to carry with you in case wedding-day jitters make you forgetful. Note any other readings you would like to be spoken by a friend or relative.

....
....
....
....
....
....
....
....
....
....
....
....
....
....
....
....
....
....
....
....
....

YOUR CEREMONY SITE

Places to consider for your wedding ceremony include, but are not limited to, churches or synagogues, hotels, restaurants, clubs, a private residence (your own or someone else's), historic homes, bed and breakfast inns, wineries, resorts, parks, public gardens, recreation areas, beaches, boats, and theme parks.

Questions to ask as you investigate prospective sites:

❧ Is the site available for decorating the day before? If not, when will it be available on the day of the wedding?

❧ Is parking adequate for the number of guests invited?

❧ Are there restrictions on photography, videography, or music? Are there adequate power sources available for these services?

❧ Will we have to rent chairs and an aisle runner? Are these available on site for a fee?

❧ May guests toss birdseed or rose petals?

❧ When may we rehearse at the site?

❧ Are there dressing rooms at the site? Rest rooms?

❧ Are there any extra fees we need to know about?

❧ If the site is a church not of your faith: May we use an officiant of another faith to perform the ceremony?

❧ If the site is a public space: Do we need a permit? Are there any restrictions such as the size of the gathering?

Prospective site #1 ....
Address..
Contact ....
Tel..
Comments...

Fee(s) $ ....

Prospective site #2 ....
Address..
Contact ....
Tel..
Comments...

Fee(s) $ ....

Prospective site #3 ....
Address..
Contact ....
Tel..
Comments...

Fee(s) $ ....

When you make your choice, enter the expense in Your Budget Worksheet on page 25.

EQUIPMENT RENTAL FOR THE CEREMONY

For rented decorations for the ceremony, see page 59.

Rental company..

Address..

Contact..

Tel...

Pick-up date........................Return date......................

Chairs: No. needed: ....Estimate $ ....

Arch   Estimate $ ....

Aisle Runner   Estimate $ ....

Kneeler   Estimate $ ....

Other................................Estimate $ ....

Total Rental Fees   Estimate $ ....

Enter expenses in Your Budget Worksheet on page 25.

PURCHASING THE WEDDING RINGS

Jeweler...

Address..

Contact..

Tel...

Date ordered .... Est. date ready....................

Bride's Ring   Price $..........................

Groom's Ring   Price $..........................

Enter expenses in Your Budget Worksheet on page 25.

WEDDING TRANSPORTATION

Securing special transportation to the church, then from church to the reception, is a practical luxury. Limousine service ensures that you and your parents will arrive in timely fashion at both the ceremony and the reception, freed from having to seek your own parking spots. Also consider the style of your wedding gown and whether it will be crushed in a smaller car.

Other transportation to consider would be renting a luxury car such as a Rolls Royce or Jaguar (with or without chauffeur), or an antique or classic car. If you are planning a car trip for your honeymoon, a rented SUV or LUV might be just the ticket to take you to church, the reception, then finally the open road.

Some brides choose a "grand entrance" for their ceremony and build a themed wedding around the drama of arriving and departing in a horse-drawn carriage or hot-air balloon. (If you choose such an option, your budget allocation for transportation may be a higher percentage than that suggested on page 23.)

Depending on the parking situation at the ceremony and reception locations, you may need to offer valet parking service for your guests.

Limo or car rental ....

Address..

Contact..

Tel...

Comments...

Estimate $ ....

Enter expense in Your Budget Worksheet on page 29.

WEDDING ATTIRE

ATTIRE FOR THE BRIDE

When shopping for a bridal gown and accessories:

❧ Allow four to six months for a custom-made gown.

❧ Be sure to ask about all alteration fees.

❧ Schedule fittings well in advance of the wedding date.

❧ Always wear the same lingerie and height of shoes you plan to wear at the wedding.

❧ Don't let yourself be pressured to purchase the head-piece, shoes, or other accessories at the same shop where you purchase your gown.

❧ Buy or make your headpiece at least a month before the wedding so you can work with your hairdresser on a suitable hairstyle.

GOWN

Store ....

Tel..

Contact ....

☐ Gown selected   Estimate $ ....

☐ Deposit date ....   Paid $ ....

                        Balance due $ ....

☐ First fitting date ....

☐ Final fitting date ....

☐ Estimated completion date ....

☐ Actual pick-up date................

                        Total $ ....

HEADPIECE AND VEIL

Store ....

Tel..

Contact ....

☐ Style selected   Estimate $ ....

☐ Deposit date ....   Paid $ ....

                        Balance due $ ....

☐ Estimated completion date ....

☐ Actual pick-up date...............

                        Total $ ....

EVERYTHING ELSE

☐ Shoes purchased $ ....

☐ Lingerie purchased $ ....

☐ Hosiery purchased $ ....

☐ Jewelry purchased $ ....

☐ Other .... $ ....

☐ Other .... $ ....

Enter expenses in Your Budget Worksheet on page 25.

ATTIRE FOR THE GROOM

Store ....

Tel..

Contact ....

☐ Suit fitted (if purchased) or reserved (date) ....

                        Estimate $ ....

☐ Suit picked up

☐ Shoes reserved or purchased

                        Estimate $ ....

☐ Shirt and tie reserved or purchased

                        Estimate $ ....

☐ Accessories reserved or purchased

                        Estimate $ ....

Enter expenses in Your Budget Worksheet on page 25.

ATTIRE FOR THE BRIDE'S ATTENDANTS

Honor attendant ....

Tel ....

☐ Dress selected   Color ....

☐ Dress fitted (date) ....

☐ Dress picked up (date) ....

☐ Shoes and accessories purchased

Bridesmaid ....

Tel ....

☐ Dress selected   Color ....

☐ Dress fitted (date) ....

☐ Dress picked up (date) ....

☐ Shoes and accessories purchased

Bridesmaid ....

Tel ....

☐ Dress selected   Color ....

☐ Dress fitted (date) ....

☐ Dress picked up (date) ....

☐ Shoes and accessories purchased

Bridesmaid ....

Tel ....

☐ Dress selected   Color ....

☐ Dress fitted (date) ....

☐ Dress picked up (date) ....

☐ Shoes and accessories purchased

Bridesmaid ....

Tel ....

☐ Dress selected   Color ....

☐ Dress fitted (date) ....

☐ Dress picked up (date) ....

☐ Shoes and accessories purchased

Bridesmaid ....

Tel ....

☐ Dress selected   Color ....

☐ Dress fitted (date) ....

☐ Dress picked up (date) ....

☐ Shoes and accessories purchased

Bridesmaid ....

Tel ....

☐ Dress selected   Color ....

☐ Dress fitted (date) ....

☐ Dress picked up (date) ....

☐ Shoes and accessories purchased

Flower girl ....

Tel ....

☐ Dress selected   Color ....

☐ Dress picked up (date) ....

☐ Shoes and accessories purchased

☐ Flower basket purchased

If shoes are to be dyed, allow four weeks.

Store ....

Tel ....

☐ Pick-up (date) ....

ATTIRE FOR THE GROOMSMEN

Best man ....

Tel..

☐ Ensemble reserved   Color...................................

☐ Pick-up date...............

Groomsman..

Tel..

☐ Ensemble reserved   Color...................................

☐ Pick-up date...............

Groomsman..

Tel..

☐ Ensemble reserved   Color...................................

☐ Pick-up date...............

Groomsman..

Tel..

☐ Ensemble reserved   Color...................................

☐ Pick-up date...............

Groomsman..

Tel..

☐ Ensemble reserved   Color...................................

☐ Pick-up date...............

Groomsman..

Tel..

☐ Ensemble reserved   Color...................................

☐ Pick-up date...............

Groomsman..

Tel..

☐ Ensemble reserved   Color...................................

☐ Pick-up date...............

Ring bearer...

Tel..

☐ Clothing selected   Color.....................................

☐ Pick-up (date)........................

☐ Shoes and accessories purchased

☐ Ring bearer's pillow purchased

Rental store ....

Tel ....

CEREMONY INFORMATION SHEET

Site ....

Address ....

Name of site manager ....

Tel ....

Decorating date and time ....

Officiant ....

Tel ....

Rehearsal date and time ....

Musician(s) ....

Contact ....

Tel ....

Vocalist ....

Tel ....

Florist ....

Contact ....

Tel ....

THE WEDDING DAY

Time guests will arrive ....

Time wedding party will arrive ....

Time ceremony begins ....

Order of procession

....
....
....
....
....
....
....
....
....
....
....
....
....

Order of recession

....
....
....
....
....
....
....
....
....
....
....
....
....

Planning Your Reception

YOUR RECEPTION SITE

Places to consider for your wedding reception include, but are not limited to, church or synagogue halls, hotels, restaurants, clubs, a private residence (your own or someone else's), historic homes, bed and breakfast inns, wineries, resorts, and the great outdoors. Some sites have full catering and beverage services; not only may these save you money, but they spare you the effort of arranging the various services yourself.

Questions to ask as you investigate prospective sites:

❧ Can you accommodate us on the date and time we want? Will we have to vacate the site at a specific time?

❧ Can the site accommodate the number of guests we anticipate? Will parking and restroom facilities be adequate?

❧ Is the site available for decorating the day before? If not, when will it be free for decorating on the day of the wedding?

❧ What extra equipment will I need to rent (tables and chairs, lighting, etc.)?

❧ Are there adequate power sources for videography and music?

❧ Do you offer catering and bartending service? If not, can you recommend a caterer who has worked on-site here?

❧ Are there any cooking and food preparation restrictions? May my caterer stop by to check the kitchen facilities beforehand?

❧ May we stop by the site as it's being prepared for another wedding reception?

❧ What is your cancellation and refund policy?

❧ Are there any insurance requirements? Union requirements? Permits needed? Security deposit?

After you make your decision, secure a contract with everything spelled out in detail.

Prospective site #1 ....

Address ....

Contact ....

Tel ....

Comments ....

Fee(s) $ ....

Prospective site #2 ....

Address ....

Contact ....

Tel ....

Comments ....

Fee(s) $ ....

Prospective site #3 ....

Address ....

Contact ....

Tel ....

Comments ....

Fee(s) $ ....

When you make your choice, enter the expense in Your Budget Worksheet on page 26.

YOUR WEDDING CAKE

Wedding cakes may be traditional or trendy; look through bridal magazines and books such as our companion book *Beautiful Wedding Receptions* for ideas before you begin interviewing bakers. It's also a good idea to have an estimate of the number of guests you expect.

Questions to ask prospective bakers or bakeries:

❧ My I taste-sample your cakes?

❧ How large a cake will I need for the number of guests I'm inviting?

❧ Do you have a portfolio of cake-decorating styles I can browse? If I find a cake I love, will the same person who decorated it do the work on my cake?

❧ Can you match the frosting to my bridal colors if I bring you a color swatch?

❧ If I choose to decorate my cake with fresh flowers, will you work with my florist?

❧ May I order one small but fancy cake "for looks" and additional sheet cakes to serve guests?

❧ (For a specific cake that strikes your fancy): What ingredients do you use?

❧ How far in advance do you bake your cakes?

❧ Do I pay extra for cake tiers, cake stand, trays, etc.?

❧ Do you deliver? Is there an additional cost for this?

❧ What is your cancellation and refund policy?

❧ How much will this (particular) cake cost per serving?

After you make your decision, secure a contract with everything spelled out in detail.

Prospective baker(y) #1 ....
Address...
Contact ....
Tel...
Possible cake flavor(s)..
Possible filling(s) ....
Possible frosting(s)..
Decoration ....
Comments ....

Fee $ ....

Prospective baker(y) #2 ....
Address...
Contact ....
Tel...
Possible cake flavor(s)..
Possible filling(s) ....
Possible frosting(s)..
Decoration ....
Comments ....

Fee $ ....

Prospective baker(y) #3 ....
Address...
Contact ....
Tel...
Possible cake flavor(s)..
Possible filling(s) ....
Possible frosting(s)..
Decoration ....
Comments ....

Fee $ ....

When you make your choice, enter the expense in Your Budget Worksheet on page 28.

CATERING AND BEVERAGE SERVICE

Because the cost of feeding your guests will probably take up the largest percentage of your wedding budget, it makes sense to choose your caterer carefully. Seek word-of-mouth recommendations from recently wedded couples as well as from your site manager.

Buying the beverages yourself (if allowed) can save you money. Look for a liquor discounter or wholesaler who will deliver. Consider the expense of additional items such as ice, cocktail napkins, bar fruit, and tools such as cocktail shakers and ice tongs. For best results, ask your bartender to keep a keen eye on portion control.

Questions to ask prospective caterers:

❧ (If not affiliated with a particular site): Can you work at my chosen reception site?

❧ Do you have photographs of your food presentation I can browse?

❧ May we stop by as you are setting up for another wedding reception?

❧ Can we review sample menus together? What do you consider your specialties?

❧ Can you also provide beverage service? May we provide our own liquor? If we provide our own wine and champagne, do you charge a corkage fee?

❧ Can you furnish rental items such as table linens, glassware, dinnerware, and serving utensils?

❧ Do you also do the clean-up? Return of rental items?

❧ How many persons will I need for wait staff? What attire will they wear?

❧ Will one of the wait staff cut the wedding cake even if it's from another baker? What do you charge per piece?

❧ Do you provide other wedding services such as decorating or entertainment?

❧ What is your cancellation and refund policy?

❧ May I see proof of liquor license and liability insurance?

After you make your decision, secure a contract with everything spelled out in detail.

Give your caterer the final guest count no less than one week before the wedding.

Prospective caterer #1 ....
Address...
Contact ....
Tel..
Comments..
Price per person .... X number of guests = ...
      Estimated food expense $ ....
      Estimated wait staff expense $ ....

Prospective caterer #2 ....
Address...
Contact ....
Tel..
Comments..
Price per person .... X number of guests = ...
      Estimated food expense $ ....
      Estimated wait staff expense $ ....

Prospective caterer #3 ....
Address...
Contact ....
Tel..
Comments..
Price per person .... X number of guests = ...
      Estimated food expense $ ....
      Estimated wait staff expense $ ....

When you make your choice, enter the expense in Your Budget Worksheet on page 28.

When calculating your food and beverage expenses, don't forget to figure in 15 to 20 percent tips for the caterer, bartender, and wait staff. Read your contract carefully to see if tipping is already included in the estimated expenses.

SAMPLE MENU #1

Caterer ....

Hors d'oeuvres ....

Courses ....

....

Entrée ....

....

....

Beverages ....

Dessert ....

Extras (condiments, butter, sugar, salt and pepper, etc.)

....

SAMPLE MENU #2

Caterer ....

Hors d'oeuvres ....

Courses ....

....

Entrée ....

....

....

Beverages ....

Dessert ....

Extras (condiments, butter, sugar, salt and pepper, etc.)

....

SAMPLE MENU #3

Caterer ....

Hors d'oeuvres ....

Courses ....

....

Entrée ....

....

....

Beverages ....

Dessert ....

Extras (condiments, butter, sugar, salt and pepper, etc.)

....

PLANNING THE MENU

Considerations to ask yourself:

❧ How much money can I afford to spend per guest?

❧ The meal: do I want breakfast, brunch, luncheon, tea, cocktails, dinner, or dessert?

❧ The service: do I want cocktails with hors d'oeuvres passed or on tables, buffet or food stations (served or self-served), or a seated and served meal?

❧ The courses: do I want hors d'oeuvres, appetizers, soup, salad, fruit and cheese, pasta, and/or dessert?

❧ The entrées: do I want beef, chicken, pork, seafood, lamb, pasta, or vegetarian? More than one entrée?

❧ Dessert: do I want several items, or cake only?

❧ Will I need to take special dietary needs into consideration for vegetarian, low-cholesterol, or kosher diets?

❧ Alcohol: do I want a full bar (open or limited), beer and wine only, wine with dinner, a champagne toast, or a specialty cocktail?

RENTAL EQUIPMENT FOR THE RECEPTION

Rental company...

Address...

Contact...

Tel...

Pick-up date.....................Return date.....................

FOR THE SITE

For rented decorations for the reception, see page 59.

When you discuss your plans with the site manager or coordinator, find out which of the following items you will need to rent separately:

	Quantity	Cost
Tent	....	....
Tables size..............	....	....
size..............	....	....
Umbrellas	....	....
Chairs	....	....
Lighting (describe).................		
	....	....
Fans or heaters	....	....
Extension cords	....	....
Other......................	....	....
	Estimate $	....

FOR FOOD AND BEVERAGE SERVICE

The items listed below are also available in disposable paper or plastic as an alternative to renting.

When you discuss your plans with your caterer, find out if you need to rent the following items separately:

LINENS	Quantity	Cost
Tablecloths (__" x __")	....	....
Tablecloths (__" x __")	....	....
Dinner napkins	....	....
Cocktail/dessert napkins	....	....

DINNERWARE	Quantity	Cost
Dinner plates	....	....
Salad/luncheon plates	....	....
Bread plates	....	....
Soup bowls	....	....
Dessert plates	....	....
Coffee cups and saucers	....	....
GLASSWARE		
Champagne flutes	....	....
Wine glasses	....	....
Water goblets	....	....
Highballs	....	....
Double rocks	....	....
Punch cups	....	....
FLATWARE		
Dinner knives	....	....
Steak knives	....	....
Butter knives	....	....
Dinner forks	....	....
Salad forks	....	....
Dessert forks	....	....
Teaspoons	....	....
Soup spoons	....	....
SERVING PIECES		
Platters	....	....
Bowls	....	....
Serving utensils	....	....
Salt and pepper shakers	....	....
Ice chest/cooler	....	....
Punch bowl	....	....
Water pitchers	....	....
Coffee maker	....	....
Electric hot plate(s)	....	....
Other......................	....	....
Estimated food and beverage rentals $		
Estimated total rental fees $		

Enter the expenses in Your Budget Worksheet on page 28.

RECEPTION INFORMATION SHEET

Site ....

Address ....

Site manager ....

Tel...

☐ Contract signed

☐ Deposit date ....   Paid $ ....

                Balance due $ ....

Decorating date and time ....

Caterer ....

Tel...

Contact ....

            Estimate $ ....

☐ Contract signed

☐ Deposit date ....   Paid $ ....

                Balance due $ ....

Begin set-up ....

Estimated departure time ....

Baker ....

Tel...

Contact ....

            Estimate $ ....

☐ Contract signed

☐ Deposit date ....   Paid $ ....

                Balance due $ ....

Delivery time ....

Musician(s) or DJ ....

Tel...

Contact ....

            Estimate $ ....

☐ Contract signed

☐ Deposit date ....   Paid $ ....

                Balance due $ ....

Begin set-up ....

Estimated departure time ....

Florist ....

Tel...

Contact ....

            Estimate $ ....

☐ Contract signed

☐ Deposit date ....   Paid $ ....

                Balance due $ ....

Delivery time ....

Enter expenses in Your Budget Worksheet on pages 26–28.

RECEPTION TIMELINE

.... Arrive at reception site

.... Form receiving line

.... Serve beverages

.... Serve food

.... Offer toasts

.... First dance

.... Cut the cake

Add entries to Your Wedding Day Timeline on page 90.

Wedding Enhancements

FLOWERS AND DECORATIONS

Filling your wedding with flowers offers many options: traditional bouquets, corsages, and arrangements from a professional florist; informal, personally arranged flowers and herbs from your garden or farmers' market; silk flowers for both bouquets and decorations; potted plants for decorations, to rent or to buy. There's no reason why you can't combine options; for example, using fresh flowers for bouquets, silk flowers for pew and chair decorations, and potted palms for your reception site.

To maximize your flower budget, think creatively. Perhaps the altar arrangements can also be used at the head reception table. Your attendants will look lovely holding single opulent flowers which are guaranteed not to upstage your bouquet. Small potted plants as table decorations can double as favors your guests can take home.

CHOOSING A FLORIST

Seek recommendations from your site manager or photographer, as well as other brides. Have swatches or photographs of your wedding colors in hand when you visit the florist's shop.

Questions to ask as you interview a prospective florist:

❧ Can you accommodate my wedding date? What time will you deliver the flowers?

❧ Do you have photographs of bouquets and floral arrangements I can browse?

❧ Can you suggest flowers that will fit my budget?

❧ What flowers will typically be in season at the time of my wedding?

❧ Do you charge a delivery or set-up fee?

❧ May I stop by beforehand as you are setting up for another wedding?

❧ Do you have other items I may rent, such as vases, urns, candelabrum, aisle standards, etc.?

❧ What is your policy for cancellations and refunds?

Prospective Florist #1 ....

Address...

Tel..

Contact ....

Comments...

....

      Flowers for ceremony, estimate $ ....

      Flowers for reception, estimate $ ....

           Total, estimate $ ....

Prospective Florist #2 ....

Address...

Tel..

Contact ....

Comments...

....

      Flowers for ceremony, estimate $ ....

      Flowers for reception, estimate $ ....

           Total, estimate $ ....

Prospective Florist #3 ....

Address...

Tel..

Contact ....

Comments...

....

      Flowers for ceremony, estimate $ ....

      Flowers for reception, estimate $ ....

           Total, estimate $ ....

When you make a decision, enter the expense in Your Budget Worksheet on page 27.

Secure a contract with everything spelled out in detail.

FLOWERS FOR THE CEREMONY AND RECEPTION

	Flower(s)	Color(s)	Estimate $	Ordered
Bouquets				
Bride	....	....	$	☐
Bride's toss-away	....	....	$	☐
Honor attendant	....	....	$	☐
Bridesmaids x..........	....	....	$	☐
Flowers for hair				
Bride	....	....	$	☐
Honor attendant	....	....	$	☐
Bridesmaids x..........	....	....	$	☐
Flower girl	....	....	$	☐
Boutonnieres				
Groom	....	....	$	☐
Best man	....	....	$	☐
Groomsmen x..........	....	....	$	☐
Ring bearer	....	....	$	☐
Fathers	....	....	$	☐
Others......................	....	....	$	☐
Corsages				
Mother of the bride	....	....	$	☐
Mother of the groom	....	....	$	☐
Others......................	....	....	$	☐
Altar	....	....	$	☐
Chair trims	....	....	$	☐
Pew trims	....	....	$	☐
Petals for flower girl's basket	....	....	$	☐
		Subtotal	$	

FLOWERS FOR THE RECEPTION

	Flower(s)	Color(s)	Estimate $	Ordered
Flowers for the cake	....	....	$	☐
Flowers for decór				
Head table	....	....	$	☐
Guest tables x..........	....	....	$	☐
Cake table	....	....	$	☐
Guest book table	....	....	$	☐
For standards	....	....	$	☐
		Subtotal	$	

Decorations to Buy, Borrow, Rent

Item	# Needed	Source	Estimate $	Purchased/Reserved
Potted plants			$	☐
Aisle standards			$	☐
Candles (size)			$	☐
(size)			$	☐
(size)			$	☐
Candelabrum, candlesticks			$	☐
Vases (size)			$	☐
(size)			$	☐
(size)			$	☐
Garden statuary, urns, etc.			$	☐
Balloons (color)			$	☐
(color)			$	☐
(color)			$	☐
Toasting glasses			$	☐
Cake knife			$	☐
Cake topper			$	☐
Flower girl's basket			$	☐
Ring bearer's pillow			$	☐
Guest book and pens			$	☐
Place card holders			$	☐
Paper table runners (color)			$	☐
Tulle (color)			$	☐
Ribbons (color/width)			$	☐
(color/width)			$	☐
(color/width)			$	☐
Other			$	☐
			$	☐
			$	☐
			$	☐
			$	☐
			$	☐
			$	☐

WEDDING FAVORS YOU MAKE

Favor ....

Number required ....✻

Materials required	Amount for one		Total amount	Estimate
....	....	X✻=	....	$..................
....	....	X✻=	....	$..................
....	....	X✻=	....	$..................
....	....	X✻=	....	$..................
....	....	X✻=	....	$..................
....	....	X✻=	....	$..................
....	....	X✻=	....	$..................
....	....	X✻=	....	$..................
....	....	X✻=	....	$..................
			Total	$..................

Date to make favors ....

Favor makers ....

....

....

....

....

....

PHOTOGRAPHY

After seeking recommendations from brides and site managers, plan to interview several photographers and ask to see their portfolios. Discuss exactly what you want in terms of formal posed photographs and informal candid shots. Ask how many exposures will be taken (the number should be approximately three times as many as you will purchase). Decide how many photographs you actually want to purchase, in what sizes, and how they will be presented (loose prints or albums).

PROPOSED SHOTS

☐ Engagement photo

☐ Candid shots of pre-wedding preparations

☐ Traditional posed shots of bride and groom only

☐ Traditional posed shots of entire wedding party

☐ Informal shots of bride and groom with their families

☐ Shots of ceremony decorations

☐ Candid shots of the ceremony

☐ Candid shots leaving the church

☐ Shots of reception decorations and cake table

☐ Candid shots of the reception and getaway

Prospective photographer #1 ....

Address..

Tel...

No. of shots proposed ....

☐ before ceremony   ☐ after ceremony

☐ during reception

Comments...

Promised date to review proofs....................................

Promised delivery date of photographs ....

Estimate $ ....

Prospective photographer #2 ....

Address..

Tel...

No. of shots proposed ....

☐ before ceremony   ☐ after ceremony

☐ during reception

Comments...

Promised date to review proofs....................................

Promised delivery date of photographs ....

Estimate $ ....

When you make a decision, enter the expense in Your Budget Worksheet on page 28.

Secure a contract with everything spelled out in detail.

VIDEOGRAPHY

When interviewing prospective videographers, ask to see actual videos of weddings he or she has taped. You may elect to receive the video in one of several ways:

❧ Raw footage of everything the videographer shot

❧ Tape edited "in camera" as the videographer shoots, i.e., camera operator selects what and what not to shoot as the day progresses

❧ Post-edited tape, in which some footage is used and other discarded

❧ Edited tape enhanced with music or decorative titles

EVENTS TO VIDEOTAPE

1..

2..

3..

4..

5..

6..

7..

8..

9..

10..

Prospective videographer #1..

Address..

Tel..

☐ raw footage   ☐ tape edited "in camera"

☐ post-edited tape   ☐ enhanced tape

Comments...

Promised delivery date of video ....

Estimate $ ....

Prospective videographer #2..

Address..

Tel..

☐ raw footage   ☐ tape edited "in camera"

☐ post-edited tape   ☐ enhanced tape

Comments...

Promised delivery date of video ....

Estimate $ ....

When you make a decision, enter the expense in Your Budget Worksheet on page 26.

Secure a contract with everything spelled out in detail.

MUSIC

DECIDING WHAT YOU WANT

For the ceremony, think about what styles of music will harmonize with your service. Ask yourself which would be more appropriate for the site: live music or recorded? Do you prefer instrumental, vocal, or a blend of both? Will you be married in a church with an organ? Can the pastor recommend an organist? For instrumental music, consider a string quartet or small brass ensemble. For vocal music, consider either a soloist or small vocal group that specializes in either sacred or popular music. Ask the musicians about their repertoire, and invite suggestions for possible numbers.

For the reception, think about your own preferences as well as those of your guests. Happily, you can probably enjoy several diverse musical styles if you wish. Plan on enjoying gentle background music for the receiving line and dining, followed by dance music. Choose a live band, disk jockey, or your favorite recorded music. If you want a special number the band doesn't know, you can play it on tape or CD.

SELECTING MUSICIANS

Prospective musician(s) #1..

Tel..

Contact..

Style of music...

☐ appropriate for ceremony

☐ appropriate for reception

Hours needed...............   Estimate $ ....

Prospective musician(s) #2..

Tel..

Contact..

Style of music...

☐ appropriate for ceremony

☐ appropriate for reception

Hours needed...............   Estimate $ ....

Prospective musician(s) #3..

Tel..

Contact..

Style of music...

☐ appropriate for ceremony

☐ appropriate for reception

Hours needed...............   Estimate $ ....

Prospective disk jockey #1..

Tel..

Music styles offered ....

....

....

Hours needed...............   Estimate $ ....

Prospective disk jockey #2..

Tel...

Music styles offered ....

....

....

Hours needed............... Estimate $ ....

Prospective disk jockey #3..

Tel...

Music styles offered ....

....

....

Hours needed............... Estimate $ ....

Estimated music expense for the ceremony

$ ....

Estimated music expense for the reception

$ ....

Total $ ....

When you make a decision, enter the expense in Your Budget Worksheet on page 28.

Secure a contract with everything spelled out in detail.

MUSIC FOR YOUR CEREMONY

Prelude, as the guests arrive and are seated

....

performed by..

....

performed by..

Processional, as the wedding party arrives

....

performed by..

Interlude(s), a pause during the ceremony

....

performed by..

....

Recessional, as the wedding party departs

....

performed by..

Postlude, as the guests depart

....

performed by..

MUSIC FOR YOUR RECEPTION

"Must-hear" numbers

....

performed by..

....

performed by..

....

performed by..

....

performed by..

....

performed by..

The bride and groom's first dance

....

performed by..

The father-daughter dance

....

performed by..

For a sing-along

....

performed by..

For a special tribute

....

performed by..

Wedding Formalities

LEGAL ISSUES

CONTRACTS

Most wedding-day crises and disappointments are caused by ambiguous contracts or lack of any written agreements. It's your right to ask for clearly written contracts from all your service providers, spelling out in detail what services you expect, estimates of the total cost including extra fees, the date of the wedding, the time of day you begin, and the cancellation policy. Get receipts for all deposits.

Secure a contract for each of these services:

- Ceremony and reception sites
- Caterer and cake baker
- Florist
- Bridal gown salon
- Photographer and videographer
- Musicians or disk jockey
- Wedding consultant

MARRIAGE LICENSE

A marriage license is issued by the state in which you will marry, granting you and your fiancé permission to marry. It requires the signatures of the bridal couple, two witnesses, and a religious or civil official who has the authority to join you in matrimony. Usually, the official will mail the license to the appropriate state or local office, but ask whether he or she will do this for you.

The requirements for a marriage license vary from state to state. Inquire at your local city or county marriage bureau, usually at the city or county clerk's office. Find out well ahead of time (at least two months before the wedding) what your state requires in terms of a blood test, health certificate, and other paperwork you may need to obtain from out of state. Licenses have an expiration date, from as many as 180 days to as few as 20, so check on this, too, and don't apply for your license too far ahead of the wedding date.

To qualify for a marriage license, you and your fiancé must apply together in person and provide the required paperwork as specified by your state. This may include:

- Birth certificate, driver's license, or other proof of age and citizenship
- A blood test and health certificate
- Legal proof of divorce or annulment in the case of a previous marriage

NAME CHANGE

Brides (and even some grooms) often elect to change their names after the wedding. Keep in mind that your marriage license should be signed with your post-wedding name, but your passport will bear your pre-wedding name until you apply to have it amended with the proper paperwork after the wedding. This is not an option if you're leaving immediately for your honeymoon, so you will be traveling under your pre-wedding name.

If you change your name, notify or amend the following:

- Driver's license, car registration
- Passport
- Post office, subscriptions
- Bank accounts, safety deposit boxes, retirement pensions, investments, property titles, insurance policies, wills, trusts
- Credit cards, business billings, loans
- Doctor, dentist, etc.
- Employment and school records
- Voter registration, telephone listing

PASSPORTS AND VISAS

If you will be traveling out of the country on your honeymoon, make sure you have a valid passport. If you don't have a passport, apply for one at least three months prior to the wedding date.

You may also need to apply for a visa to the country you will be visiting. Inquire at the appropriate consulate for an estimate on how much time it will take for your visas to be approved.

PRENUPTIAL AGREEMENT

Couples choose to sign prenuptial agreements to protect finances such as trust funds, children from previous marriages, and rights of inheritance. Young couples who have not accumulated serious assets probably don't need a prenuptial agreement.

Each state has its own laws that establish contractual regulations that govern how property is divided. Find out how your state's laws would affect you; you may find that existing laws suit your needs satisfactorily. But if you are entering marriage with considerable assets such as real estate, stocks, jewelry, art, or right of inheritance, consult with an attorney or financial planner to discuss whether you need to protect these assets.

If you have children from a previous relationship, you must look at protecting their right to inheritance, especially if you expect to inherit assets from your family.

It's very important to discuss the advisability of a prenuptial agreement openly with your fiancé. Some couples feel squeamish about discussing such "unromantic" issues. Others feel that such communication proves that they take the relationship seriously.

If you choose to proceed with a prenuptial agreement, discuss with your fiancé what you would like the contract to cover. One of you should then have his or her attorney draw up a legal contract for you to review. The other should have a different attorney review it, if necessary.

CHRISTIAN CEREMONY PROTOCOL

SEATING

- Bride's family and guests sit on the left side.
- Groom's family and guests sit on the right side.
- In a setting with two aisles, the bride's guests sit on both sides of the left aisle, the groom's on both sides of the right.
- If one family has many more guests than the other, guests may sit together.
- Parents sit in the first row.
- Grandparents and siblings sit in the second row.
- Additional rows may be reserved for other honored guests.
- Other guests are seated from front to back as they arrive and are not ushered if they arrive after the mothers are seated.

PROCESSION

- The officiant, groom, and best man stand at the altar area, facing the guests.
- Groomsmen, from shortest to tallest (in Protestant ceremonies, enter from the back; in Catholic ceremonies enter from the right of the altar area)
- Bridesmaids, individually or in pairs, from shortest to tallest, followed by:
  - Junior bridesmaids, if any
  - Brides' honor attendant
  - Ring bearer, if any
  - Flower girl, if any
  - Bride, on her father's (or other escort's) left arm
- In a setting with two aisles, use the left aisle for the procession, and the right for the recession.
- In a simple ceremony, a procession is optional.

CEREMONY

- Once they reach the first row of seats, the groomsmen proceed to stand to the right of the groom, the bridesmaids to the left of the bride, in lines, or, if there are many attendants, they may line up, alternating bridesmaids and groomsmen on each side.

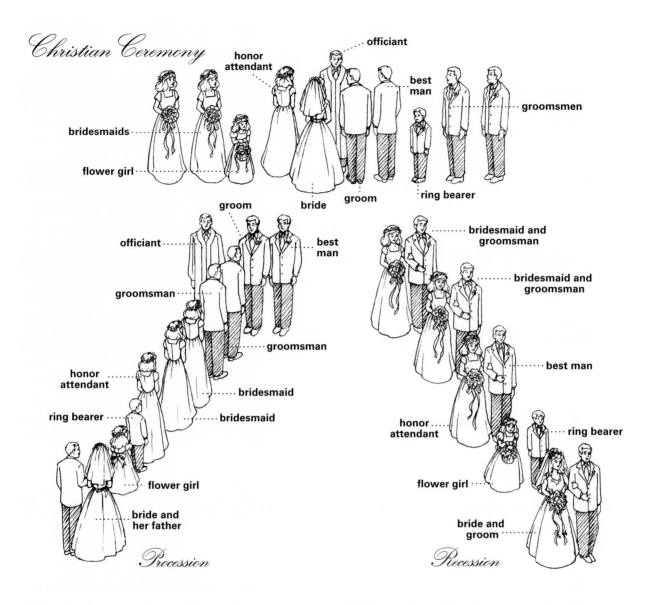

Christian Ceremony

Procession

Recession

Diagram labels (top): officiant, honor attendant, best man, groomsmen, bridesmaids, flower girl, groom, bride, groom, ring bearer

Diagram labels (procession): groom, officiant, best man, groomsman, groomsman, honor attendant, bridesmaid, ring bearer, bridesmaid, flower girl, bride and her father

Diagram labels (recession): bridesmaid and groomsman, bridesmaid and groomsman, best man, honor attendant, ring bearer, flower girl, bride and groom

❧ The ring bearer and flower girl may line up with other attendants, or may sit in the second or third row if very young.

❧ The bride stands to the left of the groom; both face the officiant.

❧ Depending on the service, the brides' father either kisses her and takes a seat in the first row, or he remains standing until a specified point in the service.

RECESSION

❧ The bride and groom turn to face the guests, the bride takes her groom's right arm, and they lead the recession.

❧ The attendants follow in reverse order of the procession, with the honor attendant escorted by the best man and each bridesmaid escorted by a groomsman.

❧ Optional: groomsmen return to the first rows to escort single guests of honor, then direct guests to the reception.

❧ Officiant, bridal couple, honor attendant, and best man meet with the officiant to sign the marriage license. Best man hands the officiant a sealed envelope with his or her fee.

❧ Wedding party may pose for photographs at the ceremony site, if desired.

JEWISH CEREMONY PROTOCOL

SEATING

❧ Bride's family and guests sit on the right side.

❧ Groom's family and guests sit on the left side.

❧ If one family has many more guests than the other, guests may sit together.

❧ Parents stand under the *chuppah* canopy throughout the ceremony.

❧ Grandparents and siblings sit in the first row.

❧ Additional rows may be reserved for honored guests.

❧ Other guests are seated from front to back as they arrive and are not ushered in after the procession.

PROCESSION

Orthodox, Conservative, and Reform processions vary according to custom and preference. Leading a formal procession:

    ❧ Rabbi and cantor (on rabbi's left)

    ❧ Bride's grandparents

    ❧ Groom's grandparents

    ❧ Groomsmen, individually or in pairs, from shortest to tallest

    ❧ Best man

    ❧ Groom, with mother on left and father on right

    ❧ Bridesmaids, individually or in pairs, from shortest to tallest

    ❧ Honor attendant

    ❧ Ring bearer, if any

    ❧ Flower girl, if any

    ❧ Bride, with mother on left and father on right

❧ In simple ceremonies, it's optional for the groom's parents and bride's mother to join the procession.

CEREMONY

❧ The bride stands to the right of the groom; both face the rabbi and cantor.

❧ The entire bridal party and parents of the bride and groom stand under or around the *chuppah*, which may stand on its own or be held aloft on poles by honored friends or relatives.

RECESSION

❧ The bride and groom turn to face the guests, the bride takes her groom's left arm, and they lead the recession, followed by:

    ❧ Bride's parents, mother on father's left arm

    ❧ Groom's parents, mother on father's left arm

    ❧ Flower girl to left of ring bearer

    ❧ Bride's honor attendant on best man's left arm

    ❧ Bridesmaids on groomsmen's left arms

    ❧ Rabbi, with cantor on left

❧ The bride and groom retire together privately in the *yichud* (seclusion), as witnesses stand outside the door. When the couple emerge, witnesses proclaim them husband and wife.

❧ At the same time, groomsmen direct guests to the reception site.

❧ Wedding party may pose for photographs at the ceremony site.

OTHER TRADITIONS

Other faiths and cultures celebrate weddings with traditions both ancient and modern. Ask a member of your clergy to explain and discuss ways you can enrich your wedding ceremony. Another resource for traditions of other faiths is *Bride's Book of Etiquette* by the Editors of *Bride's Magazine*, published by the Berkley Publishing Group, a member of Penguin Putnam, Inc. (website: www.penguinputnam.com).

Jewish Ceremony

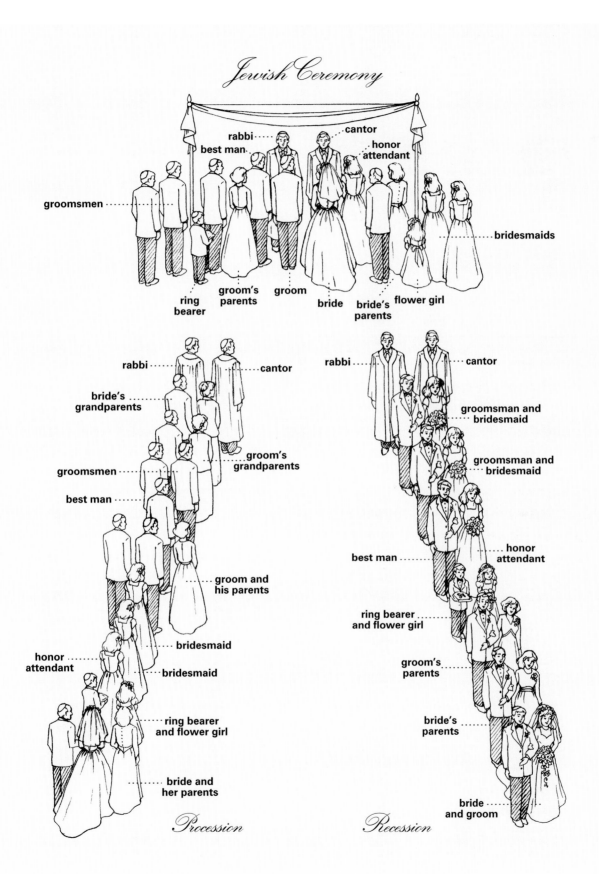

rabbi · · · · · · · · · **cantor**

best man · · · · · · · · · **honor attendant**

groomsmen · · · · · · · · · **bridesmaids**

ring bearer · · · · · · · · · **groom's parents** · · · · · · · · · **groom** · · · · · · · · · **bride** · · · · · · · · · **bride's parents** · · · · · · · · · **flower girl**

Procession

rabbi · · · · · · · · · **cantor**

bride's grandparents

groom's grandparents

groomsmen

best man

groom and his parents

bridesmaid

honor attendant

bridesmaid

ring bearer and flower girl

bride and her parents

Recession

rabbi · · · · · · · · · **cantor**

groomsman and bridesmaid

groomsman and bridesmaid

best man · · · · · · · · · **honor attendant**

ring bearer and flower girl

groom's parents

bride's parents

bride and groom

| bride's mother | bride's father | groom's mother | groom's father | bride | groom | honor attendant | bridesmaid | bridesmaid |

RECEPTION PROTOCOL

RECEIVING LINE

At large weddings, a receiving line may be the only opportunity for some guests to speak with the bride and groom and their families. The receiving line is optional at small, informal weddings.

Begin your reception line as your guests arrive. (You may elect to form your receiving line at your ceremony site if photographs were taken before the ceremony and if the site is appropriate.)

The person or persons hosting the wedding stand(s) at the head of the line. If that's your parents or your groom's parents, the mother is first, followed by the father. Next is the second set of parents, followed by the bride and groom, then the bride's honor attendant and bridesmaids. (It's optional for fathers and attendants to join the receiving line; they may circulate among the guests.) If you do not have a mother or stepmother in attendance, you may choose another female relative—a sister, aunt, or grandmother—to stand at the head of the line. If you and your groom are hosting, you may head the line.

If either set of parents is divorced, ask the father(s) to circulate among the guests. Even if the divorced parents are on friendly terms, guests may get the impression the couple is still married if both are in the receiving line.

What do you say as you greet your guests? Thank them for attending and tell them you're happy to see them. Introduce guests to your groom if he doesn't know them, adding a personal remark for context, such as "I met Paula in college," or "Please meet Pat, one of my co-workers."

SEATING

Seating is essential if you're offering a full meal, even if it's served as a buffet. Drawing up a seating plan ahead of time is an extra bit of thoughtfulness to put your guests at ease. No one need wonder "Where shall I sit?" while balancing food and drink, looking lost. Before the wedding, consider whom you think would be compatible dinner and conversational partners. Also remember guests with special needs: seat a guest with a baby nearest the door to the rest room, seat older guests away from loud noises, seat a disabled guest nearest the buffet table.

For a formal wedding, assign each guest a place card, already placed before the guests arrive. For a less formal wedding, first number each table, then arrange alphabetized place cards on a table to greet the guests as they enter; each card will have a table number, and guests may select whichever seat they like at their assigned table.

You may choose one or more of the following table arrangements for the guests of honor:

❧ The bride's or head table is a long table at one end of the room, often raised on a dais to command the guests' attention. It is set so those dining face the rest of the room. The bride and groom sit in the center, flanked by the best man and honor attendant (see illustration).

❧ The parents' table seats the parents, and the officiant and officiant's spouse (see illustration).

❧ The family table includes the newlyweds and their immediate families (see illustration).

Reception Seating

Bride's Table

Parents' Table

Family Table

FAVORS

Distributing wedding favors depends on the style of favor you buy or make. Many favors such as small frames or plants make lovely decorations at each place setting. Others may look great in a basket or bowl on the guest book table. Or ask your flower girl or junior bridesmaid to distribute favors from a basket after the meal is over.

GUEST BOOK

The guest book usually resides on a specially decorated small table where your guests can't miss it. Add a small hand-lettered or printed sign requesting they add personal messages along with their signatures. You may also ask one of your attendants to circulate through the crowd reminding guests to "sign in."

Your Personal Wedding Schedule

Your wedding planning will be easy if you start as far ahead of the wedding date as possible. Many wedding consultants and experts agree that a period of twelve months is most desirable if you want to book your first choice of sites and services. Of course, many brides plan beautiful, successful, and meaningful weddings in less time. Generally, the larger the number of guests you invite and the more formal the wedding you envision, the more time you need to arrange all the details.

Here are some tips for designing a beautiful wedding even if you only have a few months to plan:

❧ Embrace the concept "simple is elegant." Your wedding needn't be ornate or elaborate to be beautiful.

❧ Select a ceremony site that's not strictly traditional, such as a residence or an outdoor setting such as a public park or garden. For the reception, look for a clubhouse or favorite restaurant.

❧ Look for a ready-to-wear wedding gown and bridesmaids' dresses, and add a few personal touches of embellishment.

❧ Have an artistic, computer-savvy friend design and print your wedding invitations and other stationery.

❧ To save you time searching for the right musicians, consider using those you know personally, or make audio tapes or CDs of your favorite music.

❧ Celebrate your wedding early in the day and keep your menu simple.

❧ Postpone your honeymoon so you can plan it later, at your leisure.

YOUR WEDDING CHECKLIST AND COUNTDOWN CALENDAR

The month-by-month suggestions that follow are based on the assumption that you have twelve months to plan your wedding. "Month One" is the month immediately preceding the wedding. "Month Two" comes before Month One, and so on.

IF YOU HAVE NINE MONTHS TO PLAN, compress Months Twelve and Eleven into Month Nine; Months Ten and Nine into Month Eight; and Months Eight and Seven into Month Six.

IF YOU HAVE SIX MONTHS TO PLAN, compress Months Twelve through Ten into Month Six; Months Nine through Seven into Month Five; Months Six through Four into Month Four.

IF YOU HAVE THREE MONTHS TO PLAN, compress Months Twelve through Eight into Month Three; Months Seven through Four into Month Two; and Months Three and Two into Month One. One exception: mail out invitations not fewer than five weeks before the wedding.

To use the calendar, turn to the last calendar page (page 89), fill in the days of the month for the particular month of your wedding, and mark your actual wedding date. Next, fill in the dates for the months preceding your wedding month, working from back to front. Finally, fill in appointments, tasks, and personal goal dates on the appropriate days, following the suggested guidelines on the next pages.

At least once every month, compare your actual working budget against your estimated budget and make adjustments where necessary.

Your Wedding Checklist

TWELVE MONTHS BEFORE THE WEDDING

- ☐ Select the wedding date, time, and city
- ☐ Browse shops and magazines for wedding gowns
- ☐ Visit prospective ceremony and reception locations
- ☐ Decide on your wedding theme and style
- ☐ Determine how much money you have to spend (see page 22)
- ☐ Other...

ELEVEN MONTHS BEFORE THE WEDDING

- ☐ Work on your estimated budget (see page 23)
- ☐ Choose officiant
- ☐ Reserve ceremony and reception locations
- ☐ Try on various styles of wedding gowns
- ☐ Choose your wedding colors
- ☐ Other...

TEN MONTHS BEFORE THE WEDDING

- ☐ Determine maximum guest list and compile names and addresses
- ☐ Choose your attendants
- ☐ Other...

NINE MONTHS BEFORE THE WEDDING

- ☐ Begin planning the reception: interview prospective caterers, draw up sample menus, and decide on a caterer
- ☐ Interview prospective photographers and videographers, and make a decision
- ☐ Shop for bridesmaids' dresses
- ☐ Other...

EIGHT MONTHS BEFORE THE WEDDING

- ☐ Interview prospective cake bakers, sample cakes, and decide on a baker
- ☐ Interview prospective florists and make a decision.
- ☐ Select bouquets for the bridal party
- ☐ Choose your wedding gown and veil or headpiece
- ☐ Sit for engagement photograph and announce engagement in newspaper
- ☐ Other...

SEVEN MONTHS BEFORE THE WEDDING

- ☐ Select bridesmaids' dresses
- ☐ Select boutonnieres for groomsmen and corsages for family members
- ☐ Purchase all bridal attire: shoes, lingerie, stockings, jewelry, etc.
- ☐ Select accessories for bridesmaids: shoes, stockings, jewelry, etc.
- ☐ Other...

SIX MONTHS BEFORE THE WEDDING

- ☐ Complete your guest list
- ☐ Think about invitation style, gather estimates, and order samples
- ☐ Ask mothers to coordinate and select their wedding-day attire
- ☐ Research sample wedding vows
- ☐ Register for wedding gifts
- ☐ Select floral arrangements for the ceremony and reception
- ☐ Select the groom's attire
- ☐ Other...

YOUR WEDDING CHECKLIST

FIVE MONTHS BEFORE THE WEDDING

- ☐ Prepare information for your out-of-town guests
- ☐ Check your state's requirements for blood test and marriage license; make appointment for physical exam
- ☐ Purchase wedding rings
- ☐ Decide on vows or write your own; finalize ceremony details with officiant
- ☐ Begin planning your honeymoon with your fiancé
- ☐ Discuss where you will live after the wedding
- ☐ Other..

FOUR MONTHS BEFORE THE WEDDING

- ☐ Order invitations, and other stationery
- ☐ Arrange accommodations for out-of-town attendants and guests
- ☐ Decide what kind of music you want for the ceremony and reception; sample bands and disk jockeys
- ☐ Finalize arrangements with site manager(s), baker, caterer, photographer, videographer; sign contracts
- ☐ Order wedding cake
- ☐ Make decisions on honeymoon and pay deposits; arrange vacation time at your place of work
- ☐ Other..

THREE MONTHS BEFORE THE WEDDING

- ☐ Address invitations and announcements
- ☐ Prepare maps for ceremony and reception sites
- ☐ Design and print the wedding program
- ☐ Make final decision on music and sign contract(s)
- ☐ Check reservations for groom's and groomsmen's rented attire
- ☐ Finalize honeymoon plans. If you will travel out of the country, obtain passports and visas (and vaccinations if necessary)
- ☐ Other..

TWO MONTHS BEFORE THE WEDDING

- ☐ Mail invitations six weeks before wedding
- ☐ Purchase or make: birdseed packets or bubble bottles; reception favors; buy disposable cameras for reception
- ☐ Purchase accessories: ring bearer's pillow, flower girl's basket, cake knife, toasting goblets, guest book, and decorations
- ☐ Arrange final fittings for bridal gown and bridesmaids' dresses
- ☐ Get blood test and apply for marriage license
- ☐ Make plans for moving to new residence
- ☐ Other..

ONE MONTH BEFORE THE WEDDING

- ☐ Tabulate guest RSVPs and keep a running tally of head count
- ☐ Consult with hairdresser about your wedding hairstyle; make appointment for wedding day Plan what makeup look you want. Break in shoes
- ☐ Arrange for wedding day transportation
- ☐ Make rehearsal arrangements; send out invitations for rehearsal dinner. Touch base with all attendants
- ☐ Confirm reservations with all providers
- ☐ Buy gifts for the bridal party, parents, each other
- ☐ Have your hair cut a few weeks before the wedding
- ☐ If opting for a prenuptial agreement, draw up the final draft, and sign it
- ☐ Other..

See next page for the week before the wedding.

ONE WEEK BEFORE THE WEDDING

- ☐ Devise a timeline for the reception (see page 90) and notify service providers
- ☐ Provide final guest count to the caterer
- ☐ If your reception features a sit-down meal, plan seating assignments
- ☐ Touch base with your reception "director" and make sure someone is in charge of guest book and gift table
- ☐ Review final wedding day assignments with your bridal party, including decorating the ceremony and reception sites
- ☐ Pick up wedding rings and marriage license
- ☐ Arrange for someone (perhaps one of your bridesmaids) to help you dress on the wedding day
- ☐ Pick up tickets and travelers checks for honeymoon; reconfirm travel reservations
- ☐ Arrange for someone to return groom's attire after ceremony
- ☐ If moving after the wedding, fill out change of address forms and deliver to post office
- ☐ Arrange to have a manicure, facial, and massage
- ☐ Other...

A DAY OR TWO BEFORE THE WEDDING

- ☐ Rehearse ceremony with all participants
- ☐ Make your own wedding day checklist of all the items you need on hand to prepare for the ceremony, reception, and getaway
- ☐ Gather all props and accessories: ring bearer's pillow, flower girl's basket, cake knife, toasting goblets, guest book, etc.
- ☐ Give your wedding rings to honor attendants to hold until the appropriate time in the ceremony
- ☐ Make sure the groom and best man have enough cash for tipping service providers on day of the wedding
- ☐ Pack for your honeymoon and secure your luggage in your getaway car
- ☐ Pack an emergency kit for the wedding day (tissues, hairbrush, hairspray, aspirin, safety pins, extra pantyhose, etc.)
- ☐ Arrange for someone to mail announcements after the ceremony
- ☐ Other...

....
 month   year

sun	mon	tue	wed	thu	fri	sat

THINGS TO REMEMBER

....
....
....

....
month   year

sun	*mon*	*tue*	*wed*	*thu*	*fri*	*sat*

THINGS TO REMEMBER

....
....
....

sun	mon	tue	wed	thu	fri	sat

THINGS TO REMEMBER

....

....

....

....
month   year

sun	mon	tue	wed	thu	fri	sat

THINGS TO REMEMBER

....
....
....

sun	mon	tue	wed	thu	fri	sat

THINGS TO REMEMBER

....
....
....

....
month   year

sun	mon	tue	wed	thu	fri	sat

THINGS TO REMEMBER

....
....
....

sun	*mon*	*tue*	*wed*	*thu*	*fri*	*sat*

THINGS TO REMEMBER

....
....
....

....
month   year

sun	mon	tue	wed	thu	fri	sat

THINGS TO REMEMBER

....
....
....

sun	*mon*	*tue*	*wed*	*thu*	*fri*	*sat*

THINGS TO REMEMBER

....
....
....

....
month   year

sun	mon	tue	wed	thu	fri	sat

THINGS TO REMEMBER

....
....
....

....
month   year

sun	mon	tue	wed	thu	fri	sat

THINGS TO REMEMBER

....
....
....

....
month   year

sun	mon	tue	wed	thu	fri	sat

THINGS TO REMEMBER

....
....
....

....
          month   year

sun	mon	tue	wed	thu	fri	sat

THINGS TO REMEMBER

....
....
....

YOUR WEDDING DAY TIMELINE

Begin by filling in the time for "Begin ceremony procession" (at lower left) as stated on your invitation, then fill in other events backward and forward from that time, making your best estimates of the time needed.

PREPARATIONS

.... Eat a nourishing meal

.... Hair and makeup done (at least two hours before leaving for the ceremony)

.... Dress for the ceremony (at least one hour before leaving for the ceremony, unless dressing at ceremony site)

.... Leave for ceremony or photography location

AT THE CEREMONY SITE

.... If you haven't already, dress for ceremony

.... Pose for photographs now (if that is your option)

.... Groomsmen usher guests into seats

.... Assemble entire bridal party and do a head count

.... Seat family members; mothers should be seated last

.... Begin ceremony procession

AFTER THE CEREMONY

.... Distribute birdseed packets or bubble bottles to guests

.... Pose for photographs now (if that is your option)

.... Travel to reception site (if applicable)

AT THE RECEPTION SITE

.... Arrive at reception site

.... Form receiving line

.... Serve beverages (champagne, cocktails, punch, soft drinks)

.... Serve food

.... Offer toasts

.... First dance

.... Cut the cake

.... Distribute favors

THE GETAWAY

.... Toss bride's bouquet, garter

.... Say farewells and drive off

IMPORTANT NAMES AND NUMBERS

Groom ....

    Tel ....

Bride's mother ....

    Tel ....

Bride's father ....

    Tel ....

Groom's mother ....

    Tel ....

Groom's father ....

    Tel ....

Honor attendant ....

    Tel ....

Bridesmaid ....

    Tel ....

Bridesmaid ....

    Tel ....

Bridesmaid ....

    Tel ....

Bridesmaid ....

    Tel ....

Bridesmaid ....

    Tel ....

Bridesmaid ....

    Tel ....

Flower girl's parent ....

    Tel ....

Best man ....

    Tel ....

Ring bearer's parent ....

    Tel ....

Your "director" ....

    Tel ....

Indispensable friend ....

    Tel ....

Indispensable friend ....

    Tel ....

Indispensable friend ....

    Tel ....

Indispensable friend ....

    Tel ....

Wedding consultant ....

    Tel ....

Officiant ....

    Tel ....

Ceremony site manager ....

    Tel ....

Reception site manager ....

    Tel ....

Equipment rental ....

    Tel ....

Baker ....

    Tel ....

Caterer ....

    Tel ....

Florist ....

    Tel ....

Band/disk jockey ....

    Tel ....

Other musicians ....

    Tel ....

Jewelry store ....

    Tel ....

Bridal shop/dressmaker ....

    Tel ....

Hairdresser ....

    Tel ....

Men's formalwear shop ....

    Tel ....

Limousine service ....

    Tel ....

Travel agent ....

    Tel ....

WEDDING PARTIES

ENGAGEMENT PARTY

Date and Time..

Location ....

Host/Hostess ....

Tel...

Guest List:

....

....

....

....

....

....

....

....

....

....

BRIDESMAIDS' LUNCHEON

Date and Time..

Location ....

Host/Hostess ....

Tel...

Guest List:

....

....

....

....

....

....

....

....

....

....

BRIDAL SHOWER

Date and Time..

Location ....

Host/Hostess ....

Tel...

Guest List:

....

....

....

....

....

....

....

....

....

....

....

REHEARSAL DINNER

Date and Time..

Location ....

Host/Hostess ....

Tel...

Guest List:

....

....

....

....

....

....

....

....

....

....

....

PLANNING YOUR HONEYMOON

MAKING RESERVATIONS

Make reservations for travel and accommodations at least four months before the honeymoon. Begin planning earlier if you have your heart set on a popular location.

Consider the luxury of keeping close to home immediately after the reception. Reserve a bridal suite at a nearby location and plan on traveling within the next few days after you are refreshed. Or, spend your wedding night in your new home. This romantic and relaxing option offers you familiar comforts after the excitement of your special day.

If you are traveling out of the country, make reservations under the same name as on your passport, which will bear your prenuptial name.

PACKING

Select your travel attire at least two months before the wedding. It once was traditional for a bride to purchase an entire trousseau of new clothes to signify her status as a newly married woman. Many modern brides have relaxed this rule, choosing their favorite vacation clothes and perhaps adding a few new outfits for fun.

Draw up a packing list a month in advance so you won't be caught without essentials once you are away from home. Consider the weather during the season you will be visiting your destination, and think about your anticipated activities. Items such as toiletries, sunscreen, and camera film often cost considerably more in resort locations, so buy them at home before you leave.

HONEYMOON CHECKLIST

Carry these items with you in your carry-on luggage, not in your checked baggage:

- ☐ Airline or train tickets
- ☐ Itineraries, including phone numbers of accommodations (make a copy for your family)
- ☐ Traveler's checks
- ☐ List of traveler's check numbers (separate from checks)
- ☐ Emergency cash
- ☐ Passport and visas (if appropriate)
- ☐ Drivers' licenses or other legal identification
- ☐ Medications
- ☐ List of credit card numbers and phone numbers to call if cards are lost or stolen
- ☐ List of the names and phone numbers of family members you can call in case of an emergency.
- ☐ One change of clothes
- ☐ Other...

RESOURCES

BAKERY

MONTCLAIR BAKING COMPANY

Cheryl Lew
2220 Mountain Blvd. #140
Oakland, CA 04611
Tel 510-530-8052
Page 50

INVITATIONS

PRINTED AFFAIR

Leslie Bond, Marcie Redford
460 Boulevard Way
Oakland, CA 94610
Tel 510-654-9903
Fax 510-654-0016
Page 32

FLOWERS

IMPRESSIONS FLORAL DESIGN GALLERIA

2 Theater Square #136
Orinda, CA 94563-3346
Tel 925-253-0250
Fax 925-253-9946
Pages: 46, 76

PHOTO CREDITS

DIANNE WOODS

1041 Folger St.
Berkeley, CA 94710
Tel 510-841-9220

FRONT AND BACK COVERS
PAGES: (third from the top) 5, 30, 32, 46, 50, 54, 60, 76

DON FRASER

1041 Folger St.
Berkeley, CA 94710
Tel 510-841-9220

PAGE 5: (second from top) Mia Senior and Chris Untermann, private residence, San Rafael, CA; (fourth from top) Jennifer Renner and Jack Pezzolo, private residence, San Francisco, CA

PAGE 6: Rose Cardinale and Salvatore Ingrande, private residence, San Mateo, CA

PAGE 8: Jennifer Nutting and William Blando, S. F. Yacht Club, San Francisco, CA

PAGE 9: Victoria Littlejohn and Eric Schoenke, University of California Faculty Club, Berkeley, CA

PAGE 18: Shawn Elliot and Jack Marshall, Beaulieu Gardens, Rutherford, CA

PAGE 38: Mia Senior and Chris Unterman, private residence, San Rafael, CA

PAGE 39: Teri Thompson and John O'Neal, Valley Presbyterian Church, Portola Valley, CA.

PAGE 40: Melissa Chamberlain and Ken Leet, Clos Pegase Winery, St. Helena, CA

PAGE 41: Shawn Elliot and Jack Marshall, Beaulieu Gardens, Rutherford, CA

PAGE 43: Lynn Tallarida and Joe Gatti, St. Rafael's Church, San Rafael, CA

PAGE 45: Lynn Robie and Geoff Zimmerman, Captain Walsh House, Benicia, CA

PAGE 48: Mary Jane Pasha and Thomas Maxstadt, Kenwood Inn, Kenwood, CA

PAGE 52: Michelle Manick and Ken Daxer, Sonoma Golf Club, Sonoma, CA

PAGE 56: Cara Trautvetter and Clayton Cieslak, private residence, Pinole, CA

PAGE 64: Stacy Baker and Todd Morris, Old Marsh Creek Springs, Clayton, CA

PAGE 68: Stacey Getz and Robert Kertsman, Lark Creek Inn, Lark Creek, CA

PAGE 72: Jennifer Renner and Jack Pezzolo, private residence, San Francisco, CA

PAGE 95: Lyn Tallarida and Joe Gatti, St. Rafael's Church, San Rafael, CA

JEFF FIRESTONE

Firestone Photography
139 Washington Blvd.
Fremont, CA 94539
Tel 510-490-6789

Page 4: Kelly Lavery and Douglas Timm, Berkeley Marina, Berkeley, CA

DAN CATHERWOOD

Christopher Kight Photographers
2638 El Paseo Lane
Sacramento, CA 96821
Tel 916-484-1164

PAGE 5: (top) Karen Janes and Craig Coane, Cathedral of the Blessed Sacrament, Sacramento, CA

Index

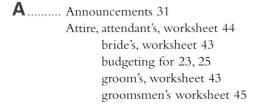

INDEX